BARNET AND HADLEY PAST

First published 2002
by Historical Publications Ltd
32 Ellington Street, London N7 8PL
(Tel: 020 7607 1628)

ISBN 0948667 78 8
British Library Cataloguing-in-Data
A catalogue record for this book is available from the British Library

Typeset in Palatino by Historical Publications
Reproduction by G & J Graphics, London EC2
Printed by Edelvives in Zaragoza, Spain

The Illustrations

The following have kindly given permission to reproduce illustrations:

Barnet Museum: *74, 94, 146, 149, 151, 152*
David C. Cumplen: *9, 71*
Jane Downey: *5, 6, 11, 12, 17, 20, 21, 22, 23, 24, 25, 26, 28, 33, 44, 45, 46, 49, 51, 54, 55, 56, 58, 61, 64, 68, 69, 76, 77, 81, 82, 89, 91, 93, 98, 99, 101, 104, 105, 107, 113, 118, 119, 123, 125, 126, 128, 132, 133, 136, 138, 141, 142, 144, 150, 155, 156, 159, 160, 161, 163, 164, 168, 173*
Mrs Giddings: *178*
Guildhall Library, Corporation of London: *40, 62, 70, 84, 87, 88, 100, 143, 167*
R.J. Harley and Middleton Press: *117*
Historical Publications: *67, 158, 170*
London Borough of Barnet: *2, 3, 7, 15, 19, 27, 29, 30, 32, 34, 35, 36, 37, 38, 39, 41, 42, 43, 47, 48, 50, 57, 59, 60, 65, 72, 73, 75, 78, 79, 85, 90, 92, 95, 96, 97, 102, 103, 106, 108, 111, 112, 114, 116, 120, 121, 122, 127, 129, 135, 137, 139, 145, 147, 148, 154, 162, 166, 169, 171, 172, 174, 175, 176, 180*
London Borough of Enfield: *66*
(in the care of) London Metropolitan Archives, Corporation of London (ACC/351/1139): *8, 52*
National Trust: *63*
Nortel: *124*
Percy Reboul: *10, 13, 16, 18, 31, 53, 80, 83, 86, 109, 110, 115, 130, 134, 140, 153, 157, 165, 177, 179*
D. Robinson: *131*
Pamela Taylor: *4, 14*

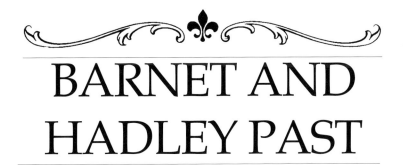

BARNET AND HADLEY PAST

Pamela Taylor

HISTORICAL PUBLICATIONS

Acknowledgements
and further reading

This book is indebted to many people, especially to those who look after or own archival material, and to those on whose researches it draws. I am particularly grateful to Jane Downey; Andrew Mussell and Hugh Petrie at Barnet Archives and Local Studies; Gillian Gear and Doreen Willcocks at Barnet Museum; and to Norma Clark, Jenny Lee Cobban, John Heathfield, Graham Javes, Hugh McLeod, Percy Reboul, Gerrard Roots and Brian Warren, all of whom have generously shared their knowledge both published and unpublished, and made the hunt infinitely more enjoyable.

The best way into the sources is via the indexes in Barnet Archives and Local Studies and in Barnet Museum.

Special mention should be made of:
Barnet Historical Society *Bulletin*, 1949 onwards
F. Cass's Histories of East Barnet, Monken Hadley, and South Mimms (1877-92)
B. Cherry and N.Pevsner *The Buildings of England. London 4 North* (1998)
J.L. Cobban and D.Willcocks, *800 Years of Barnet Market* (1999)
W. H. Gelder's various books
Hendon & District Archaeological Society *A Place in Time. The London Borough of Barnet up to c.1500* (1989)
Dong-Wook Ko, 'Society and Conflict in Barnet, Herts, 1337-1450', Birmingham PhD thesis, 1994
Victoria County History of Middlesex vol 5 (1976), which covers Barnet Mimms Side as well as Hadley.
D.Willcocks, *Barnet's History in its Street Names* (1994)

CONTENTS

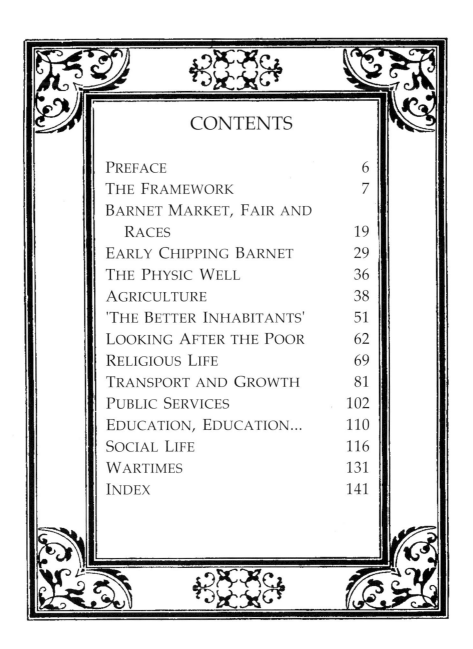

PREFACE   6

THE FRAMEWORK   7

BARNET MARKET, FAIR AND
    RACES   19

EARLY CHIPPING BARNET   29

THE PHYSIC WELL   36

AGRICULTURE   38

'THE BETTER INHABITANTS'   51

LOOKING AFTER THE POOR   62

RELIGIOUS LIFE   69

TRANSPORT AND GROWTH   81

PUBLIC SERVICES   102

EDUCATION, EDUCATION...   110

SOCIAL LIFE   116

WARTIMES   131

INDEX   141

Preface

Winter 2001/2 has been an interesting time to be writing a local history. New York may be distant from London, but the aftershock of the September 11th attack has made our own past both more recognisable and more relevant, reminding us that until very recently people in England, like everyone else across the world, lived in communities where insecurity and the fear of sudden illness and death were among the basic facts of life. Here too religion and hierarchy were controlling and interconnected forces and, among other consequences, women normally played only minor roles in public life. In all these ways our past is universal, a shared and shareable experience.

From a narrow viewpoint, though, one of the differences of the past is the minimal presence of ethnic minorities outside London and a few other major cities - and Barnet and Hadley were well outside London. Until the mid-20th century the only substantial groups of migrants in this area were Irish, making vital contributions as haymakers and navvies, but they were seasonal or transient and did not settle locally. Just west of Barnet and Hadley, what is now the Edgware branch of the Northern Line stimulated new housing in Golders Green around 1907, and then across Hendon and Edgware in the 1920s, which in turn attracted Jewish migrants, first from London's East End and then from Nazi-threatened Europe. The first Jewish families also arrived in Finchley in the 1910s, again providing, along with new housing development, a focus for a rapid rise in numbers in the 1930s. Surprisingly, neither the branch of the Northern Line beyond Finchley to High Barnet, nor the extension of the Piccadilly line to Cockfosters in the 1930s with the accompanying development of East Barnet, led to any comparable migration into Barnet and Hadley.

The cut-off point between past and present is of course subjective. Within the 20th century alone life was transformed, radically and cumulatively, by such inventions as motor and air transport, radio, television and film, telephones and the internet. All these, along with global marketing, have tended to weaken local identities and all, however skewed the distribution, are available across the planet. More locally, the introduction to Britain during the 1940s of national health and social security systems removed insecurity in an absolutely fundamental shift. Life without such safety nets has, to those who have never experienced their absence, become almost unimaginable. Already only the older generation and more recent immigrants remember a harsher past, either directly or through their parents' experiences. The cut-off point chosen here is slightly vague, but lies somewhere between 1945 and 1965.

The framework

LOCAL AUTHORITIES

This book covers Barnet and Hadley, but ignores the various historically separate places – Hendon, Finchley, Edgware, Totteridge – which were merged with them in 1965 to form the London Borough of Barnet, an entirely new composite. It also ignores Friern Barnet, which was separate from the rest of Barnet from some point before *c*.1005 up to 1965.

From 1894-1965 the area covered was that of the Urban Districts of Barnet and East Barnet Valley, and although (for reasons explained below) the northern boundary has been changeable, these were the last direct links in a connected chain of local government which had moved from the manor in the middle ages to the parish in the 16th century, and thence through various Local Boards in the 19th. Each stage threw up particular difficulties at the time, and can cause confusion now. A manor was a large estate granted at some point in the earlier middle ages to its possessor, or lord. In our area the lords, St Albans Abbey for Barnet and Geoffrey de Mandeville followed by Walden Abbey for Hadley, were large-scale owners of many estates, and always absentee; but because ecclesiastical lordship was undying, the manors avoided being divided up or weakened, and were therefore able to provide strong (residents often felt too strong) local government for their inhabitants. The original grants were made without any regard for settlement pattern. Even without Friern, the manor of Barnet was large and included various separate settlements. Some of these are still obvious today: East Barnet, Chipping or High Barnet, Arkley, but previously there were several more. Hadley, though smaller and less polyfocal, was and is also known as Monken Hadley. Cockfosters, divided between Hadley, Barnet and Enfield, was a distinct, though probably post-medieval, hamlet.

The lord of the manor was usually responsible for providing the church, and therefore, again without regard to settlement pattern or inhabitants' convenience, there was usually one church per manor. This meant that the parish – the area covered by the particular church – and the manor were coterminous. Even St John's, Chipping Barnet, an exceptional second medieval church within Barnet manor, did not obtain parochial status until 1866. In the 16th century, the Reformation caused a huge shake-up in manorial ownership, and both Barnet and Hadley passed into lay hands. The Crown also shifted most local government across from the manor to the parish, and in some areas, though not ours, manors withered away. By the 19th century the need for more wide-ranging local government was increasingly obvious, as was the unsuitability of trying to provide it through exclusively Anglican parish vestries, and as the century progressed powers were increasingly transferred to various secular boards, a process described below.

GEOLOGY AND PRE-HISTORY

Geology has been particularly important in shaping the area's settlement and agriculture. Barnet and Hadley lie firmly within the belt of heavy London Clay, with only limited areas of lighter overlay. Clay supports woodland and grass but is not much use for arable crops, and this is also true of the gravels, although they are easier to

1. A geological map of the London Borough of Barnet, taken from Hendon & District Archaeological Society, A Place in Time, *1989. The triangular spur north of Arkley is no longer in the borough.*

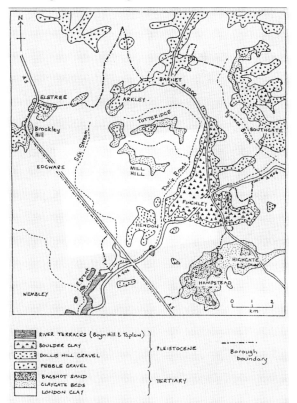

RIVER TERRACES (Boyn Hill & Taplow)

BOULDER CLAY

DOLLIS HILL GRAVEL

PEBBLE GRAVEL

BAGSHOT SAND

CLAYGATE BEDS

LONDON CLAY

PLEISTOCENE

TERTIARY

Borough boundary

clear and settle. Early settlement was usually sparse on heavy clays, and few prehistoric finds have been made in this area – a scattering of flints have surfaced, but no significant clusters. In Hadley Wood the remains of what was once a major earthwork just about survive – it was never the same after the railway was cut through it. No datable evidence has been found, but it may be Iron Age, *c*.800BC–AD43. The purpose of such barrows is not entirely clear, but they often marked boundaries rather than settlements. The Romans too were not particularly attracted to upland clay and gravel. Despite an unsupported legend that they sited a beacon on the top of Barnet Hill, several recent excavations have consistently shown that the earliest occupation there was not until the 12th–13th century.

EARLY BOUNDARIES

We all still know in which local authority we live, but this knowledge was far more important in earlier communities, where local government impinged more deeply, and where which manor court or parish church to attend was not a matter of consumer choice. The lord of the manor and the tithe-dependent parson were naturally equally keen to know the precise area of their domains. Maps are now the obvious way of recording boundaries, but this is a fairly recent response. The Ordnance Survey (OS) sheets did not exist before the 19th century, and while most areas have at least some parish and estate maps for the 18th, anything earlier is rare.

In largely illiterate societies, boundaries were beaten into the collective memory. Rogation Sunday, the 5th after Easter, became the day on which groups of parishioners perambulated the parish bounds, beating them as they went with staves, and imprinting key places with added horseplay. The bounds of Chipping Barnet were beaten six times in the 20th century, most recently in 1995, but such revivals have long been sporadic and antiquarian. In earlier periods the manor rather than the parish could be the unit of perambulation. Particularly in the 10th and 11th centuries, written boundary descriptions were sometimes appended to transfer deeds, but the survival rate from this period is extremely low.

2. *Beating the bounds of Chipping Barnet in 1933. The group is assembled outside Barnet Town Hall in Wood Street (currently the Registry Office). This had opened on the former brewery site in 1912 and replaced offices in Wood Street, built in 1889 and still surviving as Century House.*

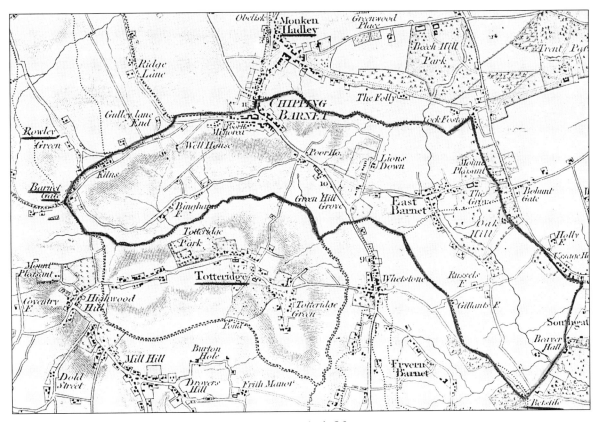

3. *The boundary of Barnet manor highlighted on the 1822 1-inch OS map.*

THE *c*.1005 BARNET BOUNDARY

Barnet is therefore exceptionally lucky in having one of these descriptions, written in Old English and appended to a deed of *c*.1005. It survives today in Brussels in a 17th-century copy of an otherwise lost 12th-century St Albans cartulary (a register of charters), and was only rediscovered in the early 1990s. The main deed was a grant by Aethelred II to St Albans Abbey of *Waetlingcaester*, or Kingsbury at St Albans, but the king also added an unnamed area of woodland, and enough of its boundary description is recognisable to know that this was more or less the later manor of Barnet.

It runs in a clockwise circuit, starting somewhere along the northern edge, and taking particular note of corners and shifts of direction. The inbetween stretches are usually simply described as the boundary with the adjacent, named, territory. The description runs: from *haewenes hlaewe* (Blue's burial mound); along the Enfield boundary; to the shire (or possibly bright) stream; to Aethelgeofu's hatch (gate); to Aescbyrht's hale

(corner); along the *Eadulfingtun* boundary; to r[or s]eodes gate; to Betstile; along the bishop's boundary; to Wakeling marsh; to Agate; to the spit of land; to and along the Brent; to the further bank; along the ditch; at Totteridge's end; along the Hendon boundary; to Grendel's Gate (now Barnet Gate); along the Shenley boundary; to Rowley; to Hadley; by the crop clearing.

It is easier to start this at the southern rather than the northern end, since the second half is straightforward. Betstile is still named on the 1822 map, and marks the sharp corner at what is now New Southgate. The next stretch, the bishop's boundary, remained intact between East and Friern Barnet until 1965, and the latter was held in the early middle ages by the Bishop of London. Wakeling marsh must have lain at the spot where a stream tributary crossed, which is known to have remained swampy until the railway mainline was put through in the 19th century. The name comes from the Waeclingas, the tribe active around St Albans (*Waetlincaester*) who also gave their name to Watling Street, and it is

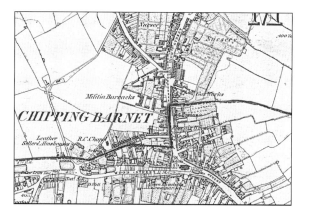

4. *The manor boundary running through Chipping Barnet, shown on the larger scale 6-inch OS map of the 1860s.*

interesting to find them so far east. Agate was at today's junction of the Great North Road and Northumberland Road; the spit is the bluff of higher ground where it reaches the Dollis Brook, a tributary of the Brent which always formed the Barnet-Totteridge boundary. We then turn north up the Hendon boundary (Hendon Wood Lane) to Barnet Gate, then sharply eastwards along a

brief stretch of the Shenley boundary to Rowley (it is interesting that Rowley rather than Arkley is named).

None of the rest is so straightforward, but Peter Kitson, who has worked extensively on Anglo-Saxon boundaries, thinks that the line was the same as the later one, with Hadley placed at the county boundary border west of Barnet High Street and *haewenes hlaewe* probably at its right angle in front of The Spires on the High Street. This then makes the Enfield boundary the Hadley Common part of the later Enfield Chase; the shire stream part of the east-flowing branch of the Pymmes Brook, perhaps with another minor tributary; and Aethelgeofu's gate the sharp south-wards turn at Cockfosters. Aescbyrht's corner must be one of the kinks further south, most probably the one between today's Vernon Crescent and Oakhill. *Eadulfington* is the later Edmonton; R / Seodes gate then has to be the sharp south-western turn at Crown Lane, Southgate (although the name of Southgate is a different formation), and thus the line runs down again to Betstile. Debate will doubtless continue, but his explanation does not run into the obvious difficulties found in other attempts.

5. *This is the point where the manor boundary turns sharply eastward across Barnet High Street. The chemist's shop was within Boundary House, whose portico was demolished in the 1940s, and the rest of the building in 1969 – although, as Boot's, it is still a chemist's. The spires of the Wesleyan chapel are now incorporated into the façade of The Spires shopping centre.*

6. Cockfosters is probably post-medieval, but standing at the Barnet boundary corner known c.1000 as Aethelgeofu's Hatch. The photograph of The Cock's forecourt was taken at the height of the cycling boom, around 1900.

Boundaries are extremely tenacious, and trying to interpret the historical Barnet and Hadley ones is best done either with the early 19th century 1-inch OS map used here, or with the earliest 6-inch edition, surveyed in the 1860s-70s before the problems the boundaries had always caused were finally addressed.

PLACE-NAMES

Even in areas of better soil and known early settlement, very few British or Roman place-names survive, since the various Germanic tribes that entered what became England from the 4th century AD renamed existing settlements as well as establishing and naming new ones. Place-name experts have a rough idea of the chronology of these name types, stretching from roughly the 4th to the 12th centuries, and ours are usually towards the later end. Hadley and Rowley, both in the c.1005 boundary description, denote woodland clearings: Hadley means heath clearing (Lysons and all who have followed him in translating as high place are wrong), and Rowley rough birch clearing. The name Barnet is usually taken to mean 'clearing by burning', which in an area such as this has an obvious logic. Nevertheless

the meaning is not entirely certain since the same name is preserved today in the form of Barnard Heath on the outskirts of St Albans, at the far end of the woodland that once stretched from there to Barnet. Although Barnet is not named in the c.1005 description, the fact that the 'bishop's boundary' (see above) already separated the later East and Friern Barnets indicates that the area name of Barnet was in existence and predated the division.

Perhaps the most interesting name in the c.1005 description is Grendelsgate, now prosaically Barnet Gate. This lies on two boundaries, of Barnet and Hendon and of Hertfordshire and Middlesex, and it is possible that the choice of Grendel, the monster of the great Anglo-Saxon epic *Beowulf*, may have something to do with boundary protection.

MONKEN HADLEY

The Barnet boundary has pushed the first known reference to Hadley back to c.1005. Nothing further is known until c.1140, when Geoffrey de Mandeville, 1st Earl of Essex, refounded Walden Abbey at Saffron Walden in Essex, and endowed it with various properties including the churches

7. *The Bell at Barnet Gate. The high-mounted gate sign on this 1930s' view hints at the spot's historic boundary position.*

and tithes of Enfield, Edmonton and South Mimms, and 'the hermitage at Hadley with all things pertaining to that place, entry, exit and common pasture for their flocks in my park in which the hermitage is situated' (for the park, later Enfield Chase, *see pp 38-41*). Although Hadley is not mentioned in Domesday Book (1086), the Survey shows that an earlier Geoffrey de Mandeville, grandfather of the 1st Earl and one of William the Conqueror's companions in 1066, was holding two large manors nearby, Edmonton and Enfield. Enfield is immediately adjacent on the east, but Edmonton included an outlier at South Mimms, immediately west of Hadley, and Hadley itself must therefore have been included within either Edmonton or Enfield, or both.

Hermitages were often deliberately isolated, but the discovery of the *c.*1005 reference probably means that there was some other habitation, however small-scale. Around 1140 Geoffrey also granted half of South Mimms to Hugh de Eu, and it is possible that the manor already had two distinct centres, a northern one in the present South Mimms village and a southern at Old Fold, which was already 'old' by 1274, and is within the same 'heath clearing' as the rest of Hadley. Equally, even hermitages needed an endowment,

and the authors of *The Story of Potters Bar and South Mimms* have suggested that Geoffrey detached part of the Old Fold section for this purpose, and that it was this separated endowment which was thereafter known as Hadley. If Peter Kitson's interpretation of the *c.*1005 Barnet boundary is right, then 'Hadley' was named west of the High Street, the Old Fold side, while everything east of the High Street was simply marked as 'along the Enfield people's boundary'. It is therefore possible that even before the hermitage existed, today's Hadley was divided between Enfield and the South Mimms outlier of Edmonton; and interesting that Cass records a deed of 1423 concerning land in 'Hadley and Monkenchurche'.

As a further complication, there had been some encroachments and enclosures on the Hadley side of Enfield Chase before the whole Chase was dismembered in 1777, and these premature enclosures – 8 acres around Mount House and 46 acres forming roughly the east side of Hadley Highstone between the Windmill and Two Brewers public houses – were counted within Enfield parish until their transfer to Hadley in 1882 and 1894 respectively for local government purposes. They were not transferred to the ecclesiastical parish of Hadley until 1922.

8. *Old Fold manor house and moat, mapped among the surrounding trees in 1726.*

9. *A tranquil view of the Pymmes Brook, c.1880.*

RIVER AND ROADS

Two branches of the Pymmes Brook join in New Barnet between the northern ends of Park and Crescent Roads, and flow southwards to the Lea. The brook was never anything more than a minor stream, a source of water but useless for transport or industry. Until the 19th century long-distance transport was easiest by water, but the absence of navigable rivers west of the Lea meant that roads north-west of London played an unusually important role.

The Romans were never the only road makers, and trackways existed long before their arrival and continued to be created as necessary afterwards. These sought well-drained ground as far as possible, and Wood Street/Barnet Road, running westward to Watling Street, is likely to be one of the earliest. Other early routes, forming an interconnecting network, include one along Longmore Avenue (until 1931 Long Street) and Cat Hill and thence eastward across the Pymmes Brook; Church Hill Road, which connected East Barnet southwards; Potters Lane and Mays Lane; and a northward route up Hendon Wood Lane, crossing Wood Street at Barnet Gate.

THE GREAT NORTH ROAD

The Romans founded London and made it the hub of a set of radiating arterial roads. Those to the north ran in the valleys either side of (and outside) our area: Ermine Street on the east and Watling Street, via Verulamium/St Albans, to the west. In the middle ages a new main road to the north was created around 1100, coming through Whetstone, up Barnet Hill and on through Hadley and South Mimms to St Albans and York. A new branch was formed from Hadley northwards via Hatfield in the 17th century and it was this, including its southern stretch, which became known as the Great North Road, the later A1. If the original road was called anything pithier than the main road to the north, the name is lost, but during the 18th century it became known as the (London to) Holyhead Road.

Road maintenance was the responsibility of the manor until the mid-16th century and the parish from then until the 19th. It was a constant problem. In 1413 Barnet High Street was 'so blocked with dung, dungheaps, pigs, pigsties and laying of timber trunks and other filth that the transit of men was much hindered and some had sustained much damage by falling with their things and harness there'. Congestion in the town was obviously an extra difficulty, but lack of maintenance was normal. Some slight help came from bequests, such as the cluster in 1447-52 when William Redehede, Richard Bates and Alice Shadd all left money to repair the stretch between Barnet and Agate. In 1347 'the upright men of the town of Barnet' were licensed by letters patent to collect tolls for five years to repair and maintain the highway from St Albans to Finchley Wood, collection to be in the town or elsewhere as convenient.

As the quantity and weight of traffic increased, matters went from bad to worse, and the idea of tolls reappeared, although this time on the privatised basis of turnpike trusts. The Whetstone Turnpike Trust was formed in 1712 to take responsibility for the stretch of the main road between the Highgate Gatehouse and Barnet Blockhouse (at Underhill) which, 'through the great traffic and droves of cattle is become so very ruinous that it is dangerous to people, horses and cattle'. In 1720 another Act extended the Trust's remit northwards to the Angel in Enfield Chase (Gannick Corner, and thus on the Great North rather than the Holyhead Road), with the rather alarming statement that the one and a half mile stretch between Hadley windmill and the Angel had never been repaired within the memory of man, because it was within Enfield Chase and its parish therefore unknown.

The situation within Barnet town continued to pose special problems, and another Act in 1763 allowed the road to be widened between Barnet Blockhouse and what is now 142 High Street (the

10. *The junction of the Great North Road with Wood Street. This picture was probably taken soon after the Middle Row in front of the church had been demolished in 1890: compare illustration 18.*

parish and county boundary), because 'by reason of the many great loads and carriages of goods and the many passengers and droves of cattle which daily pass therein [the road has] become very ruinous and in some part thereof is so narrow that carriages cannot without difficulty and danger pass by each other'. A strip of the church-yard was added into the road, but the difficulty remained.

Barnet Hill too was a difficulty. Around 1818 the trust straightened the road there, but without improving the gradient, and in 1823 the Commissioners of the Holyhead Road (whose main concern was rapid troop movement towards Ireland,

11. The Battle of Barnet obelisk was placed at the junction of the two roads to the north. On the viewer's right is the original route, coming in from St Albans via South Mimms, and on the left the newer Great North Road via Hatfield.

12. A stagecoach heading northward after successfully negotiating the narrow stretch past St John's church. The print was published by Rock & Son in 1860, by which time such coaches were rare if not non-existent.

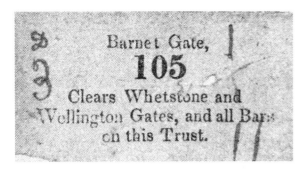

13. A Whetstone and Highgate Turnpike Trust ticket for the Barnet Gate at Underhill.

15. Charles Rea's 20th-century sketch of Underhill, with the Lower Red Lion before its 1934 rebuilding in the foreground. The sharp bend just beyond the cottages marks the amputated junction of Mays and Barnet Lanes with the Great North Road. Until the 1820s the latter climbed Barnet Hill from this point.

not the strain on horses) ordered the trust to lessen the slope. This was a major undertaking, and different strategies were suggested. In the end the idea of lowering the road into a cutting, with the pavements left on clifftops above, was rejected, and instead the old road, which climbed up from Underhill into the town at Victoria Lane, was replaced by a new causeway slightly further east, raised on earth dug from the surrounding fields, and leaving cul-de-sacs at Underhill (subsequently grassed over) and at Victoria Lane.

Soon afterwards, in 1828, the difficult South Mimms stretch of the Holyhead Road was by-passed by the New Road (since 1934 St Albans Road), driven through north-westward from the top end of Barnet High Street, and from then on the road northwards through Hadley was simply the Great North Road.

14. This extract from the 1860s OS map clearly shows the artificial causeway up into Chipping Barnet, the truncation of Underhill and Victoria Lane, and the significant junction of early lanes at Underhill.

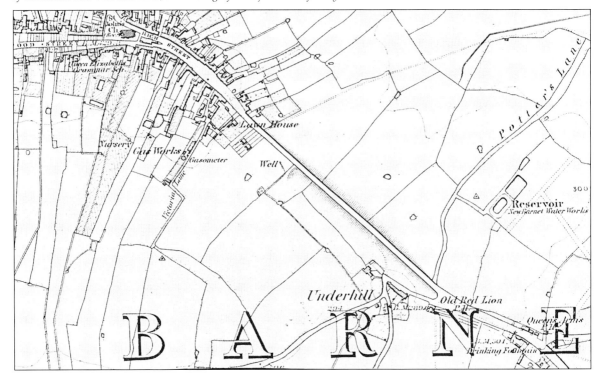

The Whetstone and Highgate Turnpike Trust was one of the better ones, but privatisation proved (not for the last time) an inadequate solution, and main roads in the London area were gradually transferred to Commissioners for the Metropolitan Turnpike Roads. The Whetstone and Highgate Trust ended in 1862. In the 1920s another wave of arterial road improvement included constructing a new route for the A1 further west to bypass the congestion of Barnet and Finchley, and the old Great North Road became the A1000.

SETTLEMENTS

Around 1005 Barnet was simply a woodland area, not yet containing a sufficiently important settlement to be worth treating as a separate manor. As with Hadley, this was still the case in 1086, and Barnet is probably concealed within the Domesday entry for the large St Albans manor called Hanstead. There were undoubtedly already settlements but they were small and scattered, and most would remain so until the fairly recent past. The amalgamation into large nucleated villages which occurred in arable areas (largely because of the requirements of communal agriculture) did not happen here.

Geology and the dreaded London Clay influenced the settlement pattern. Most of the known medieval settlements, Hadley, Barnet Gate, Arkley/Rowley, and Chipping Barnet are all on the gravel-topped plateau, and Agate too is on a hilltop. The striking exception is East Barnet, where the village centre is on the bank of the Pymmes Brook. The nearby church, though, is on a hilltop and it is possible that the original settlement migrated down to the economic opportunities provided by the river crossing. The church was usually placed in the main settlement of a manor and this one, St Mary's, is Barnet's mother church, probably founded in the mid-12th century. Roads too influenced the settlement pattern. Arkley and Grendel's Gate are both on Wood Street/Barnet Road, and Grendel's Gate and East Barnet are both at early junctions.

CHIPPING BARNET

Chipping Barnet far outgrew all the other settlements in the area, but it was a cuckoo in the nest. Taking early advantage of the new main road to the north, the abbot of St Albans planted a new settlement at an ideal trading spot, the top of a steep hill where horses and travellers might need to rest, and at the junction with Wood Street. In 1199 he obtained royal permission for a market, launching Chipping Barnet (as with Cheapside, the first element means market) on its successful career.

The new road and town altered previous patterns. In the earliest surviving manor court rolls, dating from the mid-13th century, East Barnet is regularly called simply Barnet, and Chipping Barnet Barnetley, meaning Barnet clearing and an indicator that it was secondary to East Barnet. At this stage Grendel's Gate too was still a major settlement, sometimes hosting the manor courts,

16. The 1828 new road to St Albans diverging leftwards from the old one. It had been driven through the grounds of the Green Man, separating the inn from its posting house – the derelict building shown here. Known inaccurately as the Corn Exchange, it was replaced by the current building in 1891.

17. *East Barnet village clustering in the valley rather than on the high ground near the church. The large building in the background is Clock House; note also Baker's forge.*

but both it and its road junction soon faded in importance.

As a town Chipping Barnet had one significant drawback. The site was at the extreme northern edge of the manor, hard up against the boundary with South Mimms. Things were made no simpler by the fact that the county boundary between Hertfordshire and Middlesex, defined in the 10th century but still flexible until the 12th, followed the manorial line. The St Albans manor of Barnet was therefore in Hertfordshire, but South Mimms and Hadley, although north of Barnet, were in Middlesex. In 1347 there was a major dispute between the abbot and Sir Roger de Lewkenor, lord of the manor of South Mimms. The abbot claimed that 'all the tenants and inhabitants in East Barnet and Chipping Barnet, in the county of Hertford' owed attendance at the annual view of frankpledge (the main manorial court) for Barnet, but Sir Roger claimed that 'the said tenants and inhabitants in Chipping Barnet in the county of Middlesex' owed attendance at his view of frankpledge for South Mimms. Sir Roger had a fair point, but backed down, conceding that the abbot had always exercised these rights over the tenants in the Middlesex part of the town and that he alone should continue to do so.

When the town began to expand in the early 19th century, the new development between Wood Street and the High Street was within South Mimms (Mimms Side). The old, parish-based system of local government was struggling everywhere, but Barnet's fragmentation made matters considerably worse. Permissive legislation was allowing the creation of new local boards, and in 1863 a Local Board of Health was established which covered both Barnet and Mimms Sides and Hadley.

MORE RATIONALISATION

When the Public Health Act of 1872 finally imposed Urban and Rural Sanitary Districts, existing Local Boards, including Barnet, became USDs. East Barnet was initially placed within Barnet RSD but became its own USD in 1875, and Hadley was then split between the two USDs. Both Hadley and Mimms Side were transferred to Hertfordshire in 1889.

Local government was further strengthened and simplified by the 1894 Act which created Urban and Rural Districts. Barnet and East Barnet USDs became Barnet UD and East Barnet Valley UD, and Barnet UD was extended to take in Arkley (previously in Barnet RD) in 1905 and Totteridge (not covered in this book) in 1914. Both were merged into the London Borough of Barnet in 1965, and thus lost to Hertfordshire. The London Borough's northern boundary was slightly rationalised in 1993, losing land at Rowley and gaining some at Hadley.

Barnet Market, Fair and Races

Barnet for some people still means 'hair', via the cockney rhyming slang of 'Barnet Fair', and this is some measure of the fair's former fame and importance. The fair, though, was a relative late-comer, not started until 1588. The longer history, and the greater current importance, lie with Barnet Market, which has recently celebrated its 800th anniversary.

BARNET MARKET
On 23 August 1199 King John granted the abbot of St Albans the right to hold a weekly market every Thursday in Barnet. For the king, granting such charters was a useful way of raising cash, but he and his leading tenants were also keen to stimulate trade and economic growth. Many markets were founded at this period, and those like Barnet with good locations usually flour-ished, bringing continuing profit both to the lord of the manor and to local inhabitants.

As we have seen (*p.17*), the market gave Chip-ping Barnet its name and distinctive urban char-acter. The original market place was at the top of the hill, where the road junction also provided a conveniently wide area, even larger before the church was added, probably in the 13th century. Other buildings, permanent stalls and eventually the market hall, then began to cluster against the church, forming a Middle Row with narrow streets either side. Middle Row was demolished in 1889-90, but even today it is easy to see why the stretch of High Street along the church's eastern side was long known as 'the squeeze', 'the bottleneck' and 'the narrow neck'. The market day was changed to Monday in 1588 and then to Wednesday, prob-ably in the mid-18th century. In the mid-19th the site was moved off the main road and into a space adjoining St Albans Road, and an extra market day, Saturday, was added in 1960.

The bare details, and even a visit to today's market, give little sense of the sights and smells of the medieval market place. Local people came to buy and sell food and pottery, but the market was also one of the major trading centres ringing London, selling cattle and livestock, wool and hides, corn and other grain, in quantities far beyond local needs. Here country drovers and carters sold their stock on to London dealers, and although some animals were driven on, others were fattened up and slaughtered by local butch-

18. Middle Row, with the market house at its southern end converted into a shop. Three horse-carts supply the only traffic.

ers, so that Barnet had its Shambles. It was also involved in even wider trade: in 1333 Barnet was one of the 32 manors which supplied the prior of the Hospitallers (one of the military religious orders initially founded to help recapture the Holy Land) with 380 horses, 399 oxen, 572 cows, 137 calves, 1,201 pigs, 10,353 sheep, 2,620 lambs, 40 sacks of wool, and 200 marks-weight of silver vessels for trade to merchants in Florence.

After 1539 the new lay lords of the manor were equally eager to profit, and in 1588 Queen Elizabeth (who, like King John, did a lot of this) granted a new charter renewing the market and adding an annual fair. The market house, at the southern end of Middle Row, was probably built soon afterwards: William Linacres, citizen and haberdasher of London, bequeathed £5 towards its construction in 1588, and Robert Searche of Barnet bequeathed 5s to glazing one of its windows in 1595. It was typical of its kind, timber-framed, open on the ground level, and with a large room on the upper floor, supported on twelve timber posts and reached by an external staircase. By the mid-19th century the ground floor had been walled, and it was later used as a shop. It perished with the rest of Middle Row.

The 1588 move to a Monday market seems to have been particularly helpful to Barnet's role as a meat provider. In 1592 the inhabitants of Leighton Buzzard complained that it was forestalling their own Tuesday one, and a draft parliamentary bill, never implemented, changed it back to Thursday. More seriously, the Court of Aldermen in London ordered in 1597 that 'the Wardens of the Companye of Butchers shall presentile attend Mr Recorder for his advize in a cause towching a market of Cattell kepte at Barnett to the preiudice of the markets within this City'. The London butchers then began to persuade drovers to drive the cattle in closer, Barnet protested, and in 1630 the butchers denied to the Court of Aldermen that this bypassing was making beef dearer. They also remarked that there was still plenty of corn and coal to be had there, but the meat must have been central since in 1631/2 'the restoring of Barnet Market' surfaced in the House of Lords and in 1636 the Privy Council ordered the Middlesex Justices of the Peace 'to consider the consequences of the overthrow of Barnet Market', noting that 'the object of the butchers was to discontinue Barnet Market and to establish in lieu thereof a new Monday market in West Smithfield'. All that was new in this was the day, since Smithfield had had cattle markets and fairs for centuries, but it seems to have been effective, and Smithfield soon afterwards largely superseded Barnet Market for cattle.

Pigs may have been brought in to help fill the

19. *This artist's impression, from the* Pictorial Times *of 19 April 1845, is entitled 'The fair at Barnet', but looks more like the market.*

20. *This card, showing a sheep and cattle auction in full swing, was sent by Harland & Son, auctioneers and the then owners of the market, to a client in 1905.*

gap: pig drovers were robbed *en route* to Barnet in 1682; a stretch of the hill up into the town was known as Hoggy Lane from the 17th century, and directories of 1823 and 1831 refer to the market's sales of pork and pigs. But probably by 1839, and certainly by 1850, the market had expired, killed off not only by Smithfield but also by the increase in coach traffic. Ironically, though, just at the point when we know that coaches had killed the market, the railways slaughtered coaching. The London-Birmingham railway line opened in 1838, with instantaneous effect even before the Great Northern Railway mainline through Barnet followed in 1850. Coaches rapidly vanished, and drovers, animals and markets could reclaim the streets, although the hygienic disadvantages of a town-centre location remained obvious.

At some point in the mid-19th century the lord of the manor finally sold the market, apparently to local auctioneers. By the mid-1860s the 1st edition of the Ordnance Survey shows Market Place next to the Green Man at the junction of St Albans Road, and it was presumably here that the first re-established cattle market was held in 1869 (not, as used to be thought, 1849). The present market site, almost next door, came into operation in 1874, and until the 1940s the cattle market

remained very lively. Thereafter various changes – increased regulation of slaughtering, butchers preferring to buy ready processed meat from wholesalers, fewer local farms – combined to hasten its decline, and the last cattle auction was held on 19 August 1959. The gates to the cattlepens and the weighbridge were sold, and the cleared site became a general, and still flourishing, stall market.

MARY PAYNE'S PLACE

From the mid-19th century to the mid-20th the market was more exclusively concerned with cattle than previously, and this may explain the success of a supplemental market at Mary Payne's Place, on the opposite, eastern, side of the High Street just north of Bath Place, specialising in fruit, vegetables and flowers brought in from the surrounding countryside. Also known as the Poor Man's Market, this too operated on a Wednesday, but also on Saturdays when it stayed open until 11 in the evening, allowing men who were still able to do so to collect provisions for Sunday lunch. It may have been started by ex-servicemen after World War I, and closed either in 1929, when John Swain's wanted to expand over the site, or within the following decade.

21. Mary Payne's Place, opposite the St Albans Road, in the 1920s. The bus was en route to London Bridge.

BARNET FAIR

Like the market, Barnet Fair concentrated on live-stock, particularly cattle and horses. As with all fairs, there was a big pleasure element, changing over time but including everything from a race-course through to boxing booths and helter-skelters. Although the streets must have been involved, the main fairground spread extensively along the slope around Underhill. This was part of Barnet's Common, of which some was en-closed in 1729 and the rest in 1815, a process which involved some readjustment.

The arrival of the railways (the mainline in 1850 and the suburban in 1872) encouraged increasing numbers of urban visitors bent on amusement. Many fairs in the 19th century became rather more than local residents could cheerfully bear, and many died out. In 1888 the non-resident lord of the manor petitioned the Home Secretary to close Barnet Fair, but it was still such a vital part of the local economy that he had little support. Some innkeepers reckoned to cover the whole of their annual rent with the fair takings. The Barnet Fair Defence Committee, led by W. Osborn Boys (among other posts Registrar of Barnet

County Court), pointed out, successfully, that some 40,000 cattle changed hands during each fair, and that drovers and dealers, as well as other visitors, spent considerable sums locally. 'The public were not inappreciative of [Mr Boys'] efforts. The tradesmen and licensed victuallers of the town presented him with a silver salver and testimonial, while the farmers gave him a superb

22. A card both taken and sent during the 1918 cattle fair. The sender commented that 'the fair is not so large as it was last year'.

chime clock and an address bearing the name of nearly every agriculturalist in the neighbourhood'. Although Joseph Berriman, a horse-dealer, became known as the Father of Barnet Fair, he never owned it. Instead, for over 60 years until his death in 1930 he continued a family tradition of leasing the fields from their farmers and then levying rents from the stallholders and tolls from the animal dealers.

The many pictures of the Victorian and Edwardian fairs are matched by written accounts. Billie Olney remembered her father taking her the week before the fair 'to watch those mysterious horse drawn caravans come down Barnet Hill, for they had usually come from a northern fair. They were breathtaking in their beauty, painted with strange gaudy designs and colours, and full of shining brass and ornaments. Pots and pans would be swinging on the outsides. Children and dogs swarmed everywhere'. Adults too were impressed: a *Daily Telegraph* reporter wrote in 1881: 'The high road in the immediate vicinity of Barnet Station commands an almost uninterrupted view of the broad spread of hill and dale, where the hundreds – thousands I should think it might safely be said – of horned cattle and horses are collected for buyers to pick and choose from, the cattle being separated from the horse market'.

THE CATTLE FAIR

Councillor Olney recalled that in the 1870s Wood Street was also used during the three-day fair, with booths and stalls along one side of the street, a roundabout outside the Bull inn, and the cattle on what is now Ravenscroft Gardens. And he also remembered a one-day cattle fair on the same ground in November. Amidst the enjoyment there was one painful memory, the outbreak of rinderpest in 1868 which meant (in the words of Mr Stratton) that 'hundreds of beautiful beasts Herefords and Shorthorns perished in the fields round Barnet (it was fair time) and many were buried in quick lime under [what later became] the mounds on the South Herts Golf-links'.

THE HORSE FAIR

For a child like Billie Olney 'Barnet Hill became, for a few days, all that we imagined a prairie to be, as horses of every kind, from Shetland and forest ponies, to swift racers and majestic shires, thundered down the hill and through to the fields in Barnet Lane, there to be bought and sold'. Or in the more orotund style of the *Daily Telegraph* reporter:

'I know of no other exhibition, free or otherwise, to which it was comparable.... Equine creatures from all parts of the United Kingdom, with not a few foreigners, represented the quadrupedal

23. This rare picture gives some idea of the grimmer realities underlying the fair.

24. Barnet Horse Fair. High Barnet station is in the background, with a curving fence looking remarkably like a leftover from the racecourse whose site it had taken.

party. Irish horses were there in force, with a numerically respectable contingent from Russia. Wales was to the fore with her droves of unkempt and wild mountain ponies; and drawn up in formidable array, but taking no part in the scrimmage were hundreds of sleek and powerful draught horses from the various English counties'.

The reporter does not make Billie Olney's comparison with the Wild West, but his description of the breaking-in of the wild Irish and Welsh ponies does it for him.

'Deafening yells filled the air, and in twenty places at once men might be seen engaged apparently in deadly combat with horses, the latter tugging might and main, against those who would have made them captive by means of hempen snares…threatening their assailants open-mouthed, and fighting with their fore-feet…. Whenever a horse had a chance of worsting its antagonist, a two-legged partisan would rush forward with demoniac howls, with a sounding snap flap a pink flag within an inch of its eyes, while other bipeds, with loaded whip-stocks, rattled an unearthly tattoo on the inside of their hard felt hats. Others again assailed the amazed and affrighted creatures in the rear, and slashed their flanks with stinging thongs, until, for the time, exhausted and with their strength spent,

they were brought to a standstill. Then, with a yell of triumph, the bare-throated, bare-armed, and bare-headed horse-tamers sprang on their backs, and with ear-piercing shouts of "Hi! hi! hi!" urged them at a mad gallop, apparently through the mingled crowd of horses and men, making it seem marvellous that scores of the latter were not trampled under foot.'

MISSIONARIES TO THE FAIR

The modern reader's immediate sympathy may well be for the horses, but in the mid-19th century missionaries were sent to the men. Two reports were sent to the sponsor, Captain Trotter of Dyrham Park, in 1854, full of vivid social detail, absolute devotion to the cause, and bigotry. The fair lasted from Sunday 3rd to Wednesday 6th September, and these are some highlights:

'Sat 2nd. Rev Pennyfather most cheerfully and readily granted us the loan of his lecture room in the High Street to hold our Welsh meeting on the coming Sabbath

'Lord's Day 3rd. This morning in company with Mr Lloyd Missionary to the London Welch [sic] in London distributed tracts to Welch dealers and drovers who were invited to a meeting in Barnet, and which was addressed in the Welch language by Mr Lloyd [who] spoke in a very energetical manner. To see a place for worship thus attended by plain attired Welsh people was something novel at Barnet especially the habit they wore and the language they spoke.

Mon 4th. The people conversed in the field of what they had heard on the Sabbath with much satisfaction and expressed their gratitude for the care manifested on their behalf. Very serious accidents occurred this day among the horse dealers.

Tues 5th. Assembled a large number this morning in front of an equestrian circus. The gipsies received tracts and listened to the word. One woman said theirs was a wicked life but she had been so long in it she did not know how to get out of it.

Wed 6th. On Barnet Hill this morning distributed tracts at an ale bench. Spent part of this day with Mr Lloyd in the cattle field where the preparations were going on for the races. Addressed large numbers on the bank, the people lined the railings and listened from the road. Mr Haslam also spoke but was interrupted by dealers with horses, however he continued and when order was restored the people listened. A gentleman entered into a discussion on the propriety or otherwise of attending the races.

Thurs 7th. It has been my practice to go to Barnet only the day after the fair until this year. The showmen can only be spoken to this day. The excitement is over and the work of taking down takes place. After speaking to the showmen went into a booth where five men were chatting, one being the proprietor. They offered to give us liquor. We had conversations of interest with several parties one of whom was a ginger beer and boxing booth keeper. I entered another booth where an elderly person was busily packing up with her daughter. She said to me "Oh Sir I do not like to bring up my children to this business I have put my other children to something else and I mean to do so with this one. I think much of my brother who lies in Barnet church yard – he died some years ago in a booth in this fair. I wish I was lying with him."'

THE PLEASURE FAIR

Mr Plank, who was taken to the fair as a child in 1868, remembered it stretching from today's Normandy Avenue southwards beyond and eastwards across Meadway: 'oyster and whelk stalls, whips and walking sticks were mostly sold. Steam was freely used (even then) for driving the roundabouts....The organs then (as now) were particularly blatant when *"en plein vent"'*. For Billie Olney it was the smells: '...the whelk and winkle stall outside the Old Red Lion. The pungent smell of the naphtha lights hissing and spitting over each stall. The mouthwatering smell of Barnet Fair rock...two great ropes of brown and cream sugar being thrown and twisted over two hooks, and the miracle of it ending up as a small striped stick to suck your way round the Fair with. The smell of horse dung, machine oil, and gypsy cooking'.

There were regular boxing booths at Barnet as at other fairs, and these remained popular until the bare-knuckle era ended; (for illegitimate fights *see pp 121-2*). Ex-fighters sometimes stayed around: in 1860 the legendary Tom Sayers 'was a conspicuous object during the afternoon, as he rode up and down the [race] course, ever and anon exchanging the charger on which he was mounted for a horse of a different colour'. This was a prelude to appearing with the (English) Great United States Circus, which he then took over in October 1861, and brought to Barnet in November on its initial tour. But despite initial huge audience claims, his renamed Champion Circus was far from successful, and the following year he sold it at Hendon. George Dove, a teenage bantamweight in the 1860s, moved on to become a card sharper (his pugilistic skills proving useful

25. The pleasure fair, at a time when women were still wearing ground-length skirts. The engine in front of Abbot and Barker's roundabout is titled 'Continental Scenic Railway'.

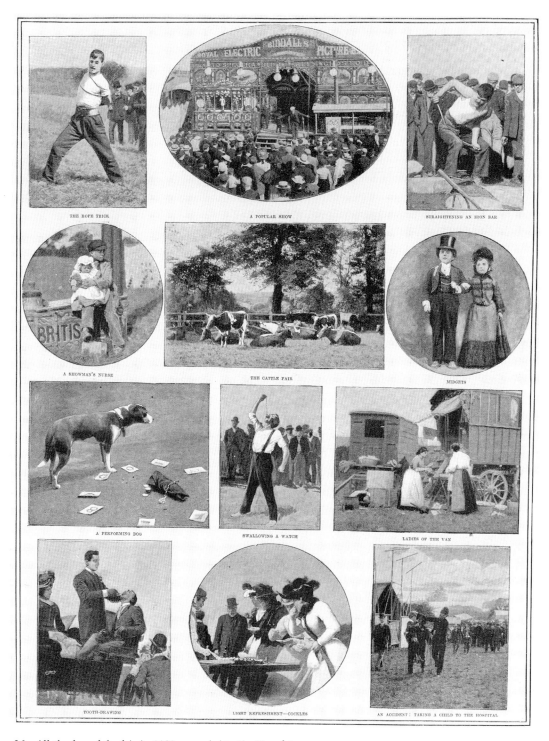

THE ROPE TRICK

A POPULAR SHOW

STRAIGHTENING AN IRON BAR

A SHOWMAN'S NURSE

THE CATTLE FAIR

MIDGETS

A PERFORMING DOG

SWALLOWING A WATCH

LADIES OF THE VAN

TOOTH-DRAWING

LIGHT REFRESHMENT—COCKLES

AN ACCIDENT: TAKING A CHILD TO THE HOSPITAL

26. *All the fun of the fair in 1902, recorded in the* Graphic.

against aggrieved victims) and enjoyed performing perched on his stool at Barnet Fair.

Hospitality booths run by former fighters became a regular feature of fairs and races in the second half of the 19th century, and particularly notable was Jesse Hatton, said in 1896 to have 'occupied the same ground at Barnet for thirty-six years'. These booths, far removed from today's hot-dog stalls, served full-scale joints of meat, poultry and game as well as the best wines, spirits and ales.

DECLINE
In the 1920s the decline in the use of horse-power largely killed the demand for horses, but (unlike Hampstead) the fairground too was vanishing. High Barnet railway line and station opened in 1872 on part of the horse fair site, and in the 1920s when the Meadway estate began to be developed over the rest, it moved west, near the other fairs in the fields between Bedford Avenue and Mays Lane. In December 1929 the *Barnet Press* reported 'Now this estate is to be developed...Barnet Fair will have to find another venue, and fields now available are fast disappearing'. The cattle fair ceased but the horse and pleasure fairs continue on fields further west, and on a modest scale.

BARNET RACES
Closely associated with the horse fair were Barnet Races, for which subscription lists and newspaper advertisements exist from 1751 onwards. The aristocracy were involved and the prizes considerable, but this was no guarantee of quality. In 1762 William Toldervy noted 'The annual horse-racing such an exhibition of bad horses, and worse riders...not to be seen at any other course in England.... 'Tis notorious, that more misfortunes generally happen at Barnet Races than at any other horse race whatever'. Perhaps this is what Horace Walpole meant when he wrote a decade later 'attended by no accident except an escape from being drowned in a torrent of whores and apprentices at Barnet races'. At this period there were also occasional one-off events, such as the one advertised in the *Public Advertiser* in May 1764: 'Thursday next a match will be run on Barnet Course between Mr Brown's bay mare Beadle-legs and Captain Harrison's bay gelding Draper for 100 guineas'.

Perhaps luckily, the course's heyday was short: even in 1793 *The Times* noted that the races had been 'miserably attended', and matters were not improved by the enclosure of the site along with

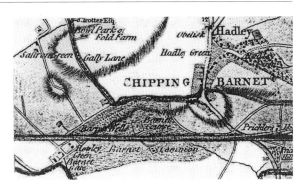

27. *The racecourse at its original site on Barnet Common is shown on various maps such as this one by John Cary in 1785.*

HERTFORDSHIRE.

Chance, late Ld. *March*'s, Covers this Season at Mr. *Topham*'s, the R.d-Lion at *Barnet*, *Hertfordshire*, at one Guinea and 1 Shilling. *Chance* is 15 Hands 1 Inch high, Master of 12 ft. free from all natural Blemishes: He was got by *Chance*, and out of a *Partner* Mare (which was the Dam of Sir *Ralph Gore*'s Grey Mare and Ld. *Portmore*'s Grey Mare, that won *Lewes* 4 Years ago, and *Guilford* 2 Years ago;) he beat *Shakefpear* over *Huntingdon*, and gave him 10 lb. Weight for the Year, and won *Nottingham* at 4 Heats, beat *Silver-leg* a Match at *Newmarket*, and run in the Chaife Match at *Newmarket*. The Money for the above Horse to be paid to Mr. *Topham*, at the Time of Covering the Mares.

Good Grass for Mares, and proper Care taken of them.

28. *Barnet's races and horse fair helped make it a centre of other equine activity, as shown in this extract from a racing guide of the mid-1750s.*

the rest of the Common in 1815, even though the course was relocated east of the Common. In 1867 the GNR laid on special trains on the mainline, but in 1871 the new suburban line and station were being built across the track. The final races, in 1870, were far from glorious, featuring only three events, of which two were walkovers, while in the third only three horses ran, of which one bolted.

GAMBLING
The fair and races attracted a lot of illegal gambling, a particular focus of the ire of the Barnet Association *(see p103)*. It noted in 1798 'that the most illegal means had been resorted to, by the promoters of the late horse races at Barnet, for raising money to be run for, by encouraging a great number of E.O. tables [gains and losses depended on a ball falling into a series of niches marked E or O], to be brought upon the race course, from London, by persons who subscribed a considerable sum to the plates, or stakes, in consequence of permission being granted them

to erect booths or tents on the race ground, in defiance of the law, and to the ruin of the unwary, whose losses were reported to have been very considerable'. The members resolved 'to take every legal means in their power, individually and collectively, to prevent the repetition of so great an evil as the introduction of this easy and commodious means of gaming to the inhabitants of this neighbourhood (particularly the lower classes), which, as it tends to their ruin, must consequently tempt them to use improper means for supplying their losses by depredations, either public or private'. They resolved to offer a reward of £10 'for the apprehension of every person who shall be convicted of keeping an E.O. table, or any other table of the same kind or use', ordered handbills to be made and distributed, and drew the Justices' attention 'to this growing evil, and desiring that they will take such steps as shall seem to them most proper for preventing its progress'.

Trying to prevent illicit activities was an expensive business. In 1799 six constables put in their account 'for attending Barnet Fair, day and night'; in 1807 the petty constable of Cashio Hundred must have had his work cut out attending Barnet during fair week to keep the peace and 'prevent all manner of gaming as well in alehouses as in other houses and places of public resort'; and in 1831 the Liberty of St Albans (in another medieval left-over, still then responsible for the former abbey estates) appointed a committee to see if the costs of policing Barnet and Northaw Fairs could be lowered, and/or passed to the respective parishes.

The boundaries between legal and illegal are of course mutable. James Ripley, the letter-writing ostler at the Red Lion, wrote disapprovingly of wagers on gentlemen riding two miles at full gallop standing upright in their stirrups. The 1756 guide to Barnet races routinely records cockfighting results.

29. *The frontispiece to James Ripley's* Select Original Letters on Various Subjects, *published in 1781.*

James Ripley, Ostler,—
at the Red Lion and Post Office Barnet
Published as the Act directs Dec.r 3. 1781.

SELECT

ORIGINAL LETTERS

ON VARIOUS SUBJECTS,

BY JAMES RIPLEY,

Now, and for Thirty Years past,

OSTLER at the RED-LION, BARNET.

LONDON:

Printed for the AUTHOR, and to be had of the following GENTLEMEN, viz.

JOHN WELLING, Esq; Jews-Harp House, Paddington.
Mr. STEPHEN ATKINSON, Merchant, Rood-Lane.
Mr. WILLIAM GOAD, Merchant, St. Thomas Apostles.
Mr. THOMAS RICHARDSON, Salesman, Gray's-Inn Lane.
Mr. BARTHOLOMEW ARLET, Stable-Keeper, Bond-Street.
Mr. HEMMING, Stable-Keeper, Curzon-Street, May-Fair.
Mr. JOHN ROBERTS, Master of the White-Horse Inn, Fetter-Lane.

M DCC LXXXI.

Early Chipping Barnet

A 16th-CENTURY DESCRIPTION

The following conversation occurs in *Dialogue against the pestilence*, written in 1573.

Civis [Citizen]: 'Wife, we have ridden ten miles this morning.'

Uxor [Wife]: 'What town is this, I pray you, sir?'

Civis: This is Barnet, whereas Samuel your son was nursed...we will not tarry now, because every inn is pestered with Londoners and carriers.... How like you this town, dame?'

Uxor: 'A pretty street; but methink the people go very plain; it is no city as I do suppose by their manners.'

30. The advertisement (from Cowing's Guide to Barnet and Neighbourhood, 1887) and the building it depicts are far from early, but both this Red Lion and today's version are successors to one of Barnet's medieval inns, known variously as the Cardinal's Hat and the Antelope.

THE RED LION HOTEL,

BARNET.

Proprietor · · C. C. F. WENGLEIN.

Masonic, Family, and Commercial Hotel.

The Grounds attached to this well known and Historical posting house, comprise fourteen acres and include extensive Pleasure Gardens with large Aviaries, Bowling Green, &c., and Private Grounds.

OCCUPATIONS

Serving travellers as well as market-goers, the town's inhabitants practised a variety of trades. Within its first 30 years (1246-75) the Barnet Court Book's copies of the manor court rolls give over 35 different surnames taken from trades and crafts. These include merchant, brewer, baker, vintner, butler (in its original sense of responsibility for a wine cellar), butcher, huckster (pedlar), spicer, skinner, tanner, fuller, tailor, weaver, draper, dyer, hat-maker, shoe-maker, cobbler, smith, brass-worker, wheeler, potter, charcoal-maker, inn-keeper, taverner, cook, courier, driver and carter. A tax return of 1334 shows the particular concentrations: eight hostelry keepers, two tavern keepers, nine bakers, four butchers, three cooks and/or fishmongers, twelve maltmongers, three tanners, two shoemakers, two smiths and fifteen brewers. There was some doubling up – all the hostelry keepers were also brewers – and most of the traders also had agricultural land.

STRESSES AND STRAINS

Although it was a town by every economic criterion, medieval Chipping had no way of separating itself from the St Albans manor of Barnet. It never acquired legal urban status, and most of its inhabitants therefore remained classed as unfree peasants, whatever their occupation. Barnet was far from unique – Westminster was the same – but the situation always caused resentment. While burgesses held their land freely and could convey it as they wished, unfree land was technically (though only technically) held at the lord's pleasure, and had to be transferred through the manor court. Transferring outside the court was the most frequent offence recorded in the Barnet rolls, and there is a splendid glimpse in 1344 of William atte Penne not only manufacturing transfer deeds but smoking them over his fire to age them. Then in the winter of 1348-9 came the Black Death, which killed between a third and a half of Barnet's population, an almost unimaginable catastrophe. Survivors, though, discovered that with land now plentiful and labour scarce the balance of economic power had shifted, and attacks on the lords' control increased. The lords responded by insisting on maintaining the *status quo*.

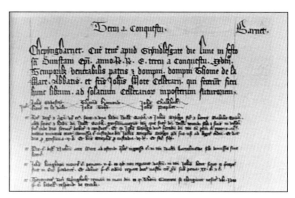

31. The record of a Barnet manor court held at 'Gryndlesgate' (Barnet Gate) in 1354. The separate court rolls were then copied into the manor court book which the abbot of St Albans managed to save in 1381.

THE PEASANTS' REVOLT

The inevitable result was the Peasants' Revolt of 1381, in which the men of Chipping Barnet played a leading role, captured for us by the horrified St Albans chronicler. On entering London on 13 June, the Kent and Essex rebels sent a message to St Albans via men from Barnet, and the next day Barnet men were again prominent in the St Albans contingent which headed to the capital and returned with the message that 'there would no longer be serfs but lords'. During the following week the rebels attacked the symbols of the abbot's lordship, broke into his prison, woods and warrens, burnt the hated court rolls and, in a startling piece of theatre, staged a mock mass, placing torn-up documents instead of bread on the tongues of the (un)faithful. They also forced the abbot to issue charters for each village: 'The people of Barnet came with bows and arrows, two-edged axes, small axes, swords and cudgels and obtained a similar charter of liberties as those of the people of St Albans, including free hunting rights, fishing rights, and rights of erecting hand mills' [milling was the lord's monopoly]. After this they demanded 'a certain book made from the court rolls' so they could burn it because it contained evidence that 'almost all the houses of Barnet were held by the rolls'. The abbot prevaricated, promising it within three weeks, and thus saved the book for posterity. The revolt was over in London on 20 June, although total suppression took longer. On 28 June royal commissioners arrived in St Albans, but there was still some resistance: '300 bowmen from the surrounding vills, especially from Barnet and Berkhamsted'. Nevertheless the rebels knew they were beaten.

On 15 July Richard II arrived in St Albans and annulled all the abbot's enforced concessions, and on 20 July received oaths of fealty from all the inhabitants of Hertfordshire.

LATER RESISTANCE

The abbot's tenants had concentrated on specific grievances rather than the more general revolutionary formulations emanating from London, but with none of these addressed, pressure soon began to rebuild. Illegal land transfers continued, and in 1417 there was another violent revolt, with royal justices eventually sent because 'the bondmen and tenants in bondage of the abbot of St Albans at Chipping Barnet have leagued together to refuse their due customs and services'. Specifically, on 19 April they had 'bound themselves by oath to support each other, refused to attend the manor court, and resisted with arms against the abbot and his officials'; in May and June the abbot sent his cellarer and bailiff, who found themselves threatened with death and mutilation. The sheriff of Hertfordshire also found it difficult to bring the rebels to trial, and the case was not finally heard until October 1418.

The abbot won, of course, but behind the rhetoric and the fines there was actually some accommodation. He had to face the impossibility of running the manor without the support of its leading families. The revolt involved both 'bondmen and tenants in bondage', an important distinction since nominally unfree land had in fact become a normal part of the land market, and men who were personally free were investing in it but irked by its restrictions. Many of those involved in 1381 were not peasants at all, but men of substantial property. The Barnet rebels in 1417 included twelve freemen, among them a citizen of London. The general solution which gradually emerged during the 15th century was the disappearance of personal unfreedom and its associated services and indignities – and refusal of such services had long been another constant in the Barnet rolls. Once personal status was no longer an issue, the actual copyhold tenure, that is land held by copy of court roll, ceased to be resented, and lasted until the 20th century.

THE HOLY TRINITY GUILD

Chipping Barnet gained its own church, probably in the 13th century, and in 1449 obtained permission to found the Guild or Chantry of the Holy Trinity within it *(see pp 69-70)*. Such guilds provided a focus of common activity and civic iden-

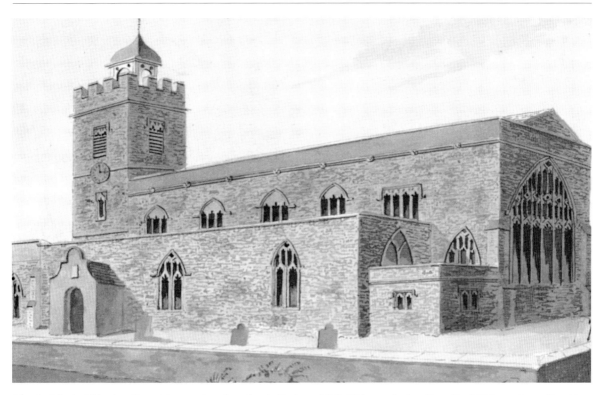

32. *St John's Chipping Barnet in a watercolour by S. Peake, c.1800. This was before its radical 19th-century alteration.*

33. *A mail coach setting out northward from London, from an engraving of 1827.*

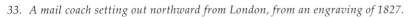

tity, particularly valuable in non-borough towns such as Barnet. They not only supported the church and chaplain but also, like the craft guilds, acted as dining, drinking and burial clubs. When the guild was wound up in 1547 its assets, including the Brotherhood House, the Brotherhood Priest's Chamber, four other houses and around 50 acres of land, were sold, and the priest, then aged 80, pensioned off.

COACHING

When all travel was on foot or by horse or horse-drawn vehicle, journeying was slow and many staging posts were needed. Chipping Barnet, eleven miles from London, was well situated, and must always have accommodated travellers. Traffic built up gradually, but there were no public stage-coaches until the 1630s and they did not become common until the mid-18th century. The Post Office began replacing post boys with a mail coach service in 1784, and started its London to Holyhead route via Barnet in October 1785. The mail coaches kept to a strict timetable, carrying travellers as well as mail sacks. By 1817, when John Hassell (whose aquatint provides this book's dustjacket) described Barnet as the 'second posting town in the kingdom, giving precedence in that line only to Hounslow', 150 coaches a day were passing through.

COLLAPSE

In 1839 Pigot's Directory prefaced its listing of the Barnet coaches with the warning 'As the Railways are opened, the number of Coaches will not only be diminished on this road, but the time of those remaining will, in all probability be altered'. By 1851 a traveller rushing past Barnet on the new Great Northern line reminisced:

'See how peacefully the place lies now...sleeping in the sun...its street is no longer noisy with the rolling of wheels, or disturbed by the crack of the coach-driver's whip. A few years since, four-horse coaches and travelling chariots streamed through Barnet like a torrent.... Now, its streets are silent, its capacious inns and posting houses are deserted, and it has subsided into a quiet out-of-the-way, country town'.

This implies that Barnet was enjoying its somnolence, but whereas motor traffic seldom benefits the settlements through which it passes, this was not the case in horse-drawn days, and towns which had depended on the trade faced great economic hardship. Nor was the problem limited to coaches. In 1839 Cox's and Flitt's carts set off

34. *The southern entry into the town, with the Woolpack, which surrendered its licence in 1931, and beyond it the Red Lion. The picture was taken before the Red Lion was halved by Fitzjohns Avenue c.1907.*

daily for London at 8am from Hadley and Wood Street respectively, while 'The Waggons of the principal land carriers, to and from London, Bedford, Biggleswade, Birmingham, Boston, Daventry, Hitchin, Leeds, Leicester, Luton, Market Street, Northampton, Nottingham, Oundle, Peterboro', Potton, Sheffield, Shefford, Silsoe, Stamford, Torrington, Towcester, and Woburn, pass regularly through Chipping Barnet and Whetstone daily, but have no particular inns or warehouses'.

Traffic did not entirely cease. There were still visitors to the market and fair, still some road travellers, and still, until roughly the 1914-18 war, carting, both local and between the Hertfordshire farms and London. Nevertheless many blacksmiths and shopkeepers must have suffered, and the area found itself heavily oversupplied with hostelries.

INNS

As the medieval lists show, there were various levels of drinking house. Alehouses were the earliest, in an extension from ordinary domestic brewing, and alewives feature regularly in the court rolls, as do the rather inadequate regulatory attempts of the manorial aleconners. Regulation increased in later centuries with the granting of

35. *At the northern entry to the town stood the Wellington and, immediately to its north, the Green Man. Both were demolished in the 1970s, and only a smaller Green Man was rebuilt.*

licences (hence licensed premises), but enforcement by local constables always allowed a wide degree of latitude. By the 18th century, when the word 'tavern' conjures the worlds of Hogarth, Richardson or Dickens, taverns sold wine and sometimes provided food and lodging while inns, the top of the range, supplied food, drink and lodging. In practice even alehouses sometimes illicitly sold spirits and accommodated guests.

With an eye to billeting, the War Office in 1756 compiled a national list of inns with beds and stabling. There were 25 along Barnet Hill and High Street, ranging in size from the Green Man, with 18 beds and stabling for 31 horses, the Red Lion (15/28), and the Harts Horns (12/50), down to the Bulls Head and Woolpack with one bed apiece and no stabling. In 1762 William Toldervy wrote that 'Chipping Barnet...consists chiefly of one street, in which are some good inns, particularly the Mitre and Red Lion'. Somewhat later, Charles Dickens (whose meal at the Red Lion had once been cut short by the news that his wife had given birth to a daughter) described Oliver Twist limping into Barnet and 'crouching on a step for some time wondering at the great number of public houses, (every other house in Barnet was a tavern, large or small)...'. And it was here that he met the Artful Dodger, probably not the only criminal in town. In 1810 the Postmaster General reported that the bags of mail had been 'stolen from the mail-box about ten o'clock on the same night, supposed at Barnet by forcibly wrenching off the lock whilst the horses were changing', and offered a reward of £100.

The inns benefited from short stops while horses were being changed, but because rutted roads

and highwaymen made travelling after dark hazardous, many south-bound coaches and their travellers spent the night there before venturing across Finchley Common; others slept at St Albans and set off early, stopping for a late breakfast at Barnet before carrying on into the city. At the height of the coaching era there were probably about thirty inns - a later sketch map produced a total of forty-three, but some were never concurrent. These are still staggering totals, not least because they exclude most of the continuation through Hadley, as well as the various taverns and alehouses.

In 1667 Pepys enjoyed 'some of the best cheesecakes that ever I ate in my life' at the Red Lion, but travellers' reports are not uniformly favourable. The Hon. John Byng recorded around 1790 that the Lower Red Lion was 'a very bad inn, with a puzzle-headed Irish waiter', the Green Man served very tough chops, and the Mitre was 'of all inns the nastiest'. There were also the usual tricks of the trade. In 1828 in *The Travellers' Oracle* William Kitchener warned those travelling by mail coach that when he had stuck to his own choice of inn at Barnet the post boy 'expressed great concern [and] candidly told me it would make a difference to him of half a guinea. Had I allowed him to take me to their own house...he should have received that sum from the Landlord'. Kitchener found this 'a very extraordinary system', but although the postal involvement strikes a distinctive note, substitute taxi drivers or street urchins and you recognise what is still in many parts of the world a commonplace.

36. William Stevens' premises, formerly the Red Lion and then the Assembly Rooms. The arched windows of the 'Great Room' and the entry to the yard (reused as the entry to Tapster Street) are still obvious today.

PITFALLS

Changing names to promote a brand identity is a recent phenomenon, but altering both names and buildings has a long history, creating plentiful traps for the unwary. Pepys' Red Lion was at the top of Barnet Hill on the eastern side; after a spell as Assembly Rooms, the site is now occupied by nos 72-6 High Street. After this Red Lion's demise its name passed to the inn half way down the hill on the western side, a medieval foundation previously called both The Cardi-

37. A picture of the Lower Red Lion at Underhill taken around 1934 while it was being replaced with its slightly repositioned successor.

nal's Hat and the Antelope. To confuse matters further, what seems originally to have been a cottage alehouse at Underhill was bought and rebuilt in the mid-18th century by the splendidly named Silver Crispin, and became known 'by the sign of the Red Lion', the Lower Red Lion (which is obvious), or the Old Red Lion (which is not). This was rebuilt in 1934 in standard interwar style.

The White Bear on the eastern side of Barnet High Street existed by 1576. It was demolished in 1831 and replaced by the short-lived Salisbury Arms and Commercial Hotel, which became a chemist's shop in 1865. Slightly further north, the Tabar was in existence by 1557, later becoming the Tabar and Pipe, and by 1769 the Royal Waggon. Only in the 1820s, after Lord Salisbury had been lured to stay there by preferential rates, did it become the Salisbury – home to so many Barnet institutions. It was rebuilt from 1928 in flamboyant Brewers' Tudor, but was demolished in 1988.

THE RED LION VERSUS THE GREEN MAN

During the coaching era the two main inns were the (Upper) Red Lion, at the southern entry to the town, and the Green Man at the northern. The Red Lion became Barnet's post office (with the landlord allegedly on one occasion throwing his breeches rather than the mail sack out into the dark), and changed post horses for free, while the Green Man lured with free sherry and sandwiches. The rivalry regularly overstepped these bounds, culminating in a court case in 1819. Thomas Newman of the Green Man had been employing 'prize fighters to prevent [Charles Bryant's] boys from approaching chaises which drove up to the Red Lion', and one of these bruisers, Richard Crouch, 'the terror of the neighbourhood', had beaten up two of the Red Lion staff because they had supplied four post-horses to Sir Robert Peel. Depressingly, although Newman was ordered to pay costs, only the fighters were imprisoned.

DISCOVERING THE EARLIER TOWN

Both the Red Lion and the Green Man survive, but on a rebuilt and diminished scale: the new St Albans Road was driven through the Green Man in 1828, and Normandy Avenue through the Red Lion around 1907. Most of the other inns have gone *(see p.88)*. Rebuilding has changed much of the High Street, although looking up above the modern shop fronts can still reveal some earlier buildings. Wood Street, though, is far less altered, and contains buildings of the 18th, 17th and, possibly, 16th centuries.

38. *Although only the twin spires and the building at the end are immediately recognisable in this north-looking view of Barnet High Street around 1900, some of the High Street's upper storeys remain relatively unchanged.*

39. *Cottages and shops in Wood Street in the late 19th century. Some cottages as well as grander houses still remain.*

The physic well

In the 17th century there was a brief possibility that Barnet would become a spa town. The curative properties of natural springs were always highly regarded (as in other countries they still are), and particularly from the 17th to early 19th centuries new springs were discovered, evaluated, and sometimes became centres of fashionable resort.

The spring on Barnet Common, first mentioned in June 1652, rapidly followed this route. In August 1653 Diana Osborne wrote of Lady Diana Holland:

> 'she has bin ill of a Paine in her stomack and has bin drinking Barnett waters and has founde her self better since. I thought they had bin soe Lately founde out that nobody had knowne what they had bin good for yet, or had ventur'd to take them'.

The water was soon agreed to be a mild purgative 'by stool and urine', due to allum or magnesium salts, and its praises were widely sung. Pepys recorded his first visit in 1664, dining first in Barnet then riding

> 'to see the Wells, half a mile off; and there I drunk three glasses and went and walked, and came back and drunk two more. The woman would have had me drunk three more; but I could not,

my belly being full – but this wrought me very well; and so we rode home... and my waters working at least seven or eight times upon the road, which pleased me well'.

Most spas were run by entrepreneurs, but perhaps because Barnet's was on the Common, it was run by the parish, which makes it all the more frustrating that the churchwardens' accounts survive so spasmodically. A well-house was constructed and by 1656, after recurrent break-ins, there was a keeper, who from 1658 was allowed to sell beer, 'strong water' and tobacco 'provided hee shuld suffer no disorder'. Those who took the waters made a donation which covered the costs, with any surplus distributed among the parish poor. In 1658 eighty benefited, but the next year bottling and selling at distant markets was temporarily halted, possibly because the spring was affected by drought. By 1663, though, the Angel and Sun in the Strand was advertising fresh Barnet well water.

In 1676, some twenty-five years after the initial discovery, John Owen, a London alderman, gave £270 to the Fishmongers' Company for investment, part of whose proceeds were to go to the well's repair. This was timely because receipts were slipping. Despite Thomas Fuller's recommendation in 1684 that 'The Water coagulateth Milk, and the Curd thereof, is an excellent Plaister for green Wounds', receipts that year were only £4, not enough to pay the keeper. In the 1660s a woman, probably the well-keeper's wife, served

40. The physic well to the right, from a watercolour of c.1790. The grand building behind is puzzling.

Pepys the water, but by the 1690s visitors served themselves. In 1689 the Queen Elizabeth School, Owen's main beneficiary, diverted his well endowment, although it made occasional disbursements thereafter. By 1724 Defoe noted that the well, 'formerly in great request, being very much approved by physicians', was 'almost forgotten'.

Some of the reasons are obvious from Celia Fiennes' account of her visit in 1697, written in her usual inimitable style. She set out from Barnet, which

'seemes to be a very sharpe air, its a large place and the houses are made commodious to entertain the Company that comes to drink the waters, which certainly if they be at paines to go once and see would have but little stomach to drink them.... I stood at the lowest step above the water to look into it, its full of leaves and dirt and every tyme they dip it troubles the water, not but what they take up and let stand looks clear but I could not taste it...it appears not to be a quick spring as Tunbridg or the Spaw or Hamsted waters, which have all fine stone basons in which you see the springs bubble up as fast, and by a pipe runs off as clear and fast...'.

Because the spring is slow-running the water was more likely to collect debris and be cloudy, but there were probably other reasons for the decline. The fashionable crowd may have enjoyed Chipping Barnet's facilities but not the windswept common, particularly if purgation was rapid. Equally, since fashion demands exclusivity, Barnet, like Hampstead, may have been too accessible to the lower orders. Local residents had access as part of their commoning rights, rights enshrined when the surrounding part of the Common was enclosed in 1729.

The well was cleared and repaired in 1796, and the problem of the debris was solved around 1808 by building an enclosing arched chamber and adding a pump, but other difficulties remained. Dr William Trinder of Arkley, author of a range of treatises and sermons, was a passionate advocate of the Barnet well, presumably with some success since his book extolling its virtues, *The English Olive Tree...with miscellaneous remarks on the prevention and cure of various diseases, gout, rheumatism, diabetes etc*, went through three editions. (The year of the first is unknown, but a second enlarged edition came out in 1802 and a third in 1812.) The book included his scientific analysis of the well's water, and claimed that it cleansed the system, cleared the skin, cured hangovers, and helped flagging appetites for both food and sex. By then the salts could be pur-

TO THE

TOWNSHIP OF BARNET, HARTS.

GENTLEMEN,

The ancient celebrity of your medicinal spring of water, on Barnet Common (which formerly made your town so much a place of resort, that, according to report, not less than thirty carriages, for hire, were kept for the convenience of the company attending the well), has induced me to think it worthy of public attention, and to dedicate to you the result of some experiments tried in this year on the water, that sufficiently show its characteristic properties. But I am sorry to observe, that the well is not now so much sheltered from the air and weather, as it was in the year 1809; and therefore, through the want of fixity in the component elements of the water, it has much degenerated from its former virtues, and even become weaker in its properties than the mineral-well water in the neighbouring house.

In the year 1800, it was slightly sulphureous both in smell and taste, till the vapour, by standing in the open air, had exhaled. Then, many persons felt a glow of the whole body at drinking it; but now it is not so much perceptible. Then, an equal quantity of the well-water and new milk made good whey; but now, to form whey, two thirds of water must be added to one of milk.

Earnestly hoping, both for your benefit and the public good, that the Barnet well water may soon be restored to its former well-deserved estimation,

I remain, Gentlemen,

Your most obedient and very humble servant,

W. M. TRINDER.

Rowley Green,
Aug. 31, 1812.   F 2

41. *William Trinder's preface to the 1812 edition of his book.*

chased from a local chemist, thus helpfully reducing the required amount of water to half a pint. Nevertheless in the 1812 edition Dr Trinder noted that the well was now less sheltered than in 1800 and that as a result the water's powers had 'much degenerated'.

Perhaps unsurprisingly, the well-house was demolished in 1840, and after a horse had fallen down the steps the entry was filled in. In the 1920s Walter Bell noticed the pump and a nearby ladder-head in a field on Well-house Farm, descended the ladder and rediscovered the chamber. This feat aroused considerable interest, not least because the farm was on the verge of development. In October 1927 *The Times* reported that the Wellhouse estate of some 180 dwellings was being built, and that the well's historic interest would be commemorated by 'a new brick structure with fountains, appropriate garden walks and flower beds, and two approaches to be named Well Road and Pepys Crescent'. The street-names are there, but the plans seem to have been modified by the time the present mock-Tudor well-house was built in 1937. Beneath this curious superstructure, though, still lies the original chamber, one of the very few to have survived unaltered.

Agriculture

WOODLAND

London Clay is better suited to woodland or pasture than to the more demanding arable cultivation. Around 1005 Barnet was simply being treated as a woodland area attached to a manor in St Albans *(see p. 9)*, and references to the woods of Southaw (at Barnet Gate and named in contrast with fairly distant Northaw) and Osidge and Monkenfrith (meaning monks' wood), both on Barnet's eastern edge, continued to abound in the manor records. The 'Barnet Wood', though, which occurs in other abbey records, refers not to Barnet but to today's Bernard Heath, on the north-eastern outskirts of St Albans. Histories based on corn-growing areas tend to treat woodland as marginal, but since trees supplied the essential material for all building and fuel, and woods the grazing for everything from the lord's deer and horses to the peasant's pigs, it was in fact a vital and highly prized resource.

ENFIELD CHASE

Enfield Chase is the most obvious local example. Geoffrey de Mandeville's park recorded in 1086 was probably the later Old Park in Enfield, smaller and further east, but by *c.*1140 the hermitage at Hadley was within his grandson's park which can therefore be identified with the later Enfield Chase, a huge enclosure covering almost 8,350 acres shortly before dismantlement in 1776. The park passed from the de Mandevilles to the Bohun earls of Essex and thence in 1399 to the Crown, and was a favourite royal hunting ground for Elizabeth I and the early Stuarts. At the same time the inhabitants of the surrounding manors and parishes, including Hadley and Old Fold but not Barnet, had always had commoning rights of pasturing animals and taking wood, as well as a tendency to poach the royal deer.

Protecting the various conflicting interests was always fraught. In 1588 William Kimpton, lord of the manor of Hadley, had to answer to the Crown for allegedly overcommoning (exceeding his allocation) and indulging in unlicensed build-

42.   The Hadley section of the Enfield Chase map of 1776. Note the corruption of 'Monken' to 'Monkey'.

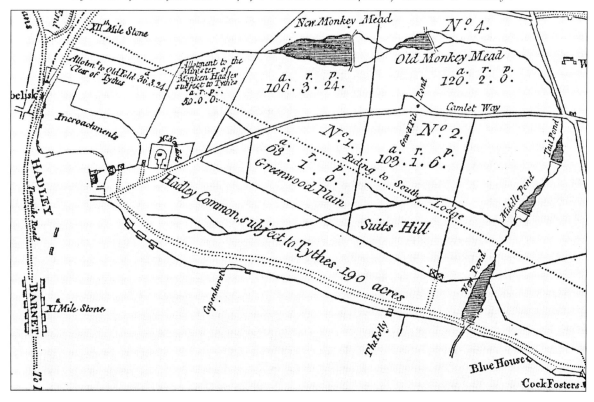

43. The coat of arms of William Kimpton, Citizen and Merchant Taylor of London.

ing. On the former he claimed, interestingly, that 'the Manor or Lordship of Hadley in auncient tyme was knowen by the name of the heremytage of Hadley', that it had passed with other rights from the dissolved abbey of Walden, and that by custom ten cattle and about twenty to forty sheep were his reasonable common of pasture. In 1652, during the Commonwealth, it was proposed that the Chase 'be sold for ready money', with 240 acres allotted to Hadley, and although nothing wholesale happened various parcels were sold. In July 1659 the inhabitants of Hadley joined with those of Enfield, Edmonton and South Mimms in threatening to destroy the new houses and enclosures which were diminishing their commoning rights.

The Chase was mapped periodically between 1636 and 1776, but not earlier. Hadley's village centre and church were outside the park in 1636 and, unlike the hermitage, had presumably always been so; but some of the grand houses radiating out along today's Common edges were started before it was disemparked, and the 1776

survey marks a thirty-odd acre block between the Common and the Great North Road at the Highstone as [irrecoverable] 'incroachments'. These were the eight acres around Mount House and the larger Highstone enclave which remained part of the parish of Enfield until the late 19th century (*see p. 12*).

The Restoration in 1660 made little difference to the Chase since neither Charles II nor his Hanoverian successors showed much interest in it. The energetic 1st Duke of Chandos leased the Rangership from at least 1728 to 1744 and tried improvements in line with the new thinking of the Agricultural Revolution, but with little success. He was not helped by poachers who 'come in open day to kill the deer and cut down all the timber', underkeepers indulging in illicit trade in deerskins, and noblemen's gamekeepers hunting illegally with their own packhounds. Meanwhile the agricultural reformers were increasingly strident. 'Enfield Chase', wrote Arthur Young in 1770, 'so large a tract of waste, so near the capital within reach of London, as a market and as a dunghill, is a real nuisance to the public'. Finally, by an Act of 1777 the Chase was dismantled since 'in its present state [it] yields very little profit or advantage either to the King's Majesty, or to the said Freeholders and Copyholders or their Tenants, in comparison of what it might do if the same was divided and improved'. The king kept over 3,000 acres but most of the rest was allotted to the surrounding parishes in proportion to their commoning rights. Among the lesser beneficiaries, Hadley received 240 acres, and Old Fold nearly 37.

Fifty of Hadley's acres were set aside to replace parish tithes (the tax which supported the parson) and became Glebe Farm, while the rest became Hadley Common, with 213 stints allotted to local householders. New regulations in 1799 gave each occupier of more than three acres in the parish a stint for cattle, but forbade horses, pigs, bulls or sheep. As late as 1925 600 cows and horses (though still no sheep) were grazed there, but although stints remain in theory, increased motor traffic and the cost of manning the cattle gates after the Second World War mean that the rights are no longer exercised. The gates survive, but the Common and Wood (the wooded eastern end) are now entirely used for recreation. Such was the fusion of Hadley manor and parish that the common was always held by the churchwardens in trust for the manor's free- and copyholders. The churchwardens still hold the legal title, but

44. *A solitary cow on Hadley Common between the two World Wars.*

45. *The Chase gate at Monken Hadley village with its keeper's hut and keeper, probably in the 1920s.*

since 1981 the Common has been managed by curators under a committee of fifteen local residents. Financial maintenance now comes from the surrounding local authorities.

In line with the 1777 Act's intention, some parts of the former Chase were cleared for agriculture, but not at Hadley. Sooner or later large areas also went to developers, including part of the Crown allotment developed by Charles Jack from the 1880s as an estate he named Hadley Wood, unhelpfully since it had never been part of Hadley. The real Hadley's inhabitants remained immovable, and apart from the railway the 190 acres are still intact.

MANORIAL COMMONS

Commons were the most extensive part of the manorial waste, a term covering all the land not included in direct cultivation. The manorial inhabitants had rights of grazing and wood collection on the commons (as in the Chase), and these were vital resources, especially for landless or near landless cottagers.

HADLEY GREEN

Again like the Chase, common land came under attack from agricultural reformers in the 18th century, and then from would-be developers. Hadley Green, otherwise known as the Old Common and, when the Battle of Barnet was fought there in 1471, as Gladmore Heath, always lay west of the Chase. In the early 19th century the lord of Hadley manor was eager to enclose it, but the vestry took him to court in 1815 and 1818, won, and secured the green as a permanent open space.

BARNET COMMON

A map of Barnet Common, undated but drawn between 1652 and 1729, shows that it covered the whole area between Wood Street on the north, Mays Lane on the south and west, and Victoria Lane, the forerunner of Barnet Hill, on the east. Such extensive grazing not only benefited smallholders but also accommodated the large numbers of livestock for the market and fair. Nevertheless in 1729 the Duke of Chandos, the lord of

46. The north-east corner of Hadley Green, with Wilbraham's almshouses in the background. Delivery carts, such as this one from Smith's bakery in Hadley, were driven through ponds both to clean the horses' feet and to shrink metal rims back onto wooden wheels.

An **A C T** *for* **Incloſing** Part of a Common *called* Barnett Common, *belonging to* the Manor *of* Chipping Barnett *in the County of* Hertford, *and for* **Veſting** *a certain annual* Rent-Charge *in* **Truſtees** *f the Benefit of the* Poor *of the Pariſh of* Chipping Barnett *for ever.*

Whereas there is a large Waſte of Ground or Common, called *Barnett* Common, containing by Eſtimation, ſeveral Hundred Acres, Parcel of the Manor of *Chipping Barnett*, in the County of *Hertford*, of which Manor the moſt Noble *James* Duke of *Chandos* is Lord.

And whereas the ſaid *James* Duke of *Chandos*, the Tenants of the ſaid Manor, and moſt of the Pariſhioners and Perſons who have any Right of Commoning and Depaſturing of Cattle in or upon the ſaid Waſte or Common, or have any other Right or Intereſt therein, being extreamly ſenſible of the great and heavy Charge and Burthen the Poor of the ſaid Pariſh of *Chipping Barnett* are to the ſaid Pariſhioners, who pay towards the Poors Rate of the ſaid Pariſh, which, if Part of the ſaid Waſte or Common was incloſed and improved, and a certain annual Rent, or Sum of Money, charged on ſuch incloſed Ground, for the Benefit of the Poor of the ſaid Pariſh, would be in ſome
A   meaſure

47. *The start of the Barnet Common Enclosure Act, 1729.*

the manor, gained permission to enclose 135 acres at the eastern end. (The otherwise excellent book on spas by Osborne and Weaver mentions an earlier Act of 1716 but this is a ghost in their machine, confusing the regnal years 2 George II and 2 George I.) The duke's ostensible reason was that he 'and most of the Parishioners and Persons who have any Right of Commoning and Depasturing of Cattle in or upon the said Waste or Common' wished to lower the burden of the poor rate by putting a rent charge on the 'inclosed and improved' land. In fact commons enclosure normally swelled the number of the poor, but this one went rapidly ahead and the Chandos charity was duly created. The rest of the Common was enclosed in 1815.

RAVENSCOURT PARK

As well as commons and greens there were other patches of manorial waste, particularly along the wide roadside verges. One stood opposite Barnet Common, on the north side of Wood Street by the Black Horse inn, with a pond much used by drovers. In 1880 Thomas Smith, developer of the adjacent Ravenscourt Park estate, offered to pay for converting this into a park, and the last piece of Barnet's manorial wasteland vanished.

48. *Ravenscourt Park c.1900. Although the park remains, the pond has gone.*

GENERAL ENCLOSURE

In fertile arable areas the entire landscape was transformed in the 18th century when the old open arable fields of strip agriculture were progressively enclosed into smaller parcels. In Barnet and Hadley there is little or no sign that open fields ever existed, and they are conspicuous by their absence from the earliest surviving court rolls, for Barnet in the 1240s. Instead, clearances for agriculture were turned immediately into small enclosed fields or crofts, even though plenty of these were initially used for arable. A Barnet court roll of 1247 records transfers of 'land', meaning arable: six acres lying between Agate (east of the Great North Road) and 'le Bruggelond', and ten acres next to Potters Lane. A description of a holding in 1360 details thirty acres in ten or twelve crofts, nearly all enclosed with hedges, and west or south of the Common: several abutted Mays Lane, at least one was next to Barnet Lane, and another stretched from Southaw Wood down to the Dollis Brook. The abbots' difficulties in extracting labour services, including threshing, from their Barnet tenants shows that they too were growing corn. Nevertheless, this was never a good corn-growing area, and some of the purchasers at Barnet Market were probably local.

MILLS

Grown or bought, the corn had to be ground, and since grains were the dietary staple (with no potato alternative until the 17th century), ground in considerable quantities. While watermills were invented well before 1066, they required substantial rivers, but windmills, in existence from the 12th century, did well on high hills and plateaus. They were also one of the lord of the manor's monopolies, operated on lease by millers, so their number was limited, and the peasant had always to use his lord's mill.

Barnet manor's sole medieval mill stood at Agate, the spur of high land still visible at the junction of the Great North Road and Northumberland Road. The site of the medieval mill at Hadley is uncertain. By the early 17th century, with the manorial monopoly broken, there were two, one just north of the modern Dury Road, which gave its name to Mill Corner and the Windmill Inn, and the other on Beacon Hill near the site of Mount House. Both were within Enfield Chase, and both had gone by the mid-18th century. West of the Great North Road, Isabel Frowyk, lady of the manor of Old Fold, had a mill by 1289 which was probably sited between the

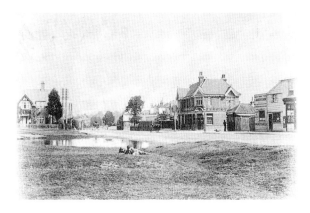

49. *The Old Windmill pub at the northern end of Hadley Green, pictured soon after it replaced an earlier building in 1900. The original pub, there by the 17th century, was next to a windmill.*

manor house and today's Christ Church. It or a successor was sold with the manor in 1639, but there are no later references. Another mill was built on Hadley Green in the early 19th century, but had gone before 1900. The only surviving mill is at Arkley *(ill. 51)*; this was built in 1806 and continued in use until the First World War.

POTTERY AND BRICKS

The local clay was highly suitable for pottery. A possibly 12th-century pottery kiln has been excavated at Dyke Cottage, Arkley, which made a wide range of cooking pots, jars, jugs, bowls and storage vessels. The pottery which has been found on sites at the top of Barnet Hill (and thus near the market where it was undoubtedly traded), also predominantly cooking pots, jugs and bowls, is somewhat later, probably 13th-century. Although it is of the general South Hertfordshire

50. *A medieval cooking pot, now in Barnet Museum, made at the Arkley kiln.*

51. Arkley mill c.1900 (see p. 43).

Grey Ware type, some at least was probably made locally. Potters Lane (in New Barnet) is so-named in 1247, and in 1290 the Barnet court roll records Christina le Potter, who 'entered a close of the lord and claims to have the right to take clay for making pots for life by paying 4d a year'.

Clay that is good for pottery is also good for bricks. The 17th-century map of Barnet Common marks 'brick kiln. Mr Ducks' just west of 'Round about Lane' (now Rowley Green Road), and although this one had gone, all the 19th -century OS maps show a concentration of brickworks and kilns slightly further west in Arkley, around Barnet Gate. The brickfield on the site of Oakfield Avenue in East Barnet was one of those which contributed to its own demise.

GRASS
Many crofts were probably always used for pasture. The animals sold at Barnet Market and Fair always needed extensive grazing, and some of Barnet's considerable concentration of butchers sometimes had to look further afield, as witness the quaintly phrased item in the *Barnet Press* for 18 September 1869: 'A Stray Sheep. – A sheep was

lost, from a field in Ridge, last week. The sheep, which was the property of Mr Anstee, butcher, of High Street, Barnet, has not since been heard of'.

Additionally, as horse-powered London's grass and hay needs expanded, even areas of better soil converted in the 17th and 18th centuries from arable to grass. In 1768 Arthur Young reported that cultivation between Barnet and London was 'all grass', with rents from £2-£3 per acre, although from Barnet to Mimms they dropped to 12s (60p) per acre.

This was a highly efficient economy, and the carters who carried the hay down to London returned laden with manure. In the 1790s London stable dung was sold at 2s (10p) a cartload, night soil and horse bones were 6s a load, soot 8d (3.5p) a bushel (although the chimney sweeps tended to 'spice' it with ash), the scrapings of sheep trotters, calves' feet and cow heels 8s a quarter, hogs hair 15s a cart load, leather, dust and shreds 2s 8d a sack, and so on, with the cost per load to Hendon 6s, South Mimms 10s, and Barnet presumably somewhere in between. All these exchanges of course benefited not only the local fields and farmers but also the innkeepers, blacksmiths and others. And not only along the main road to the north, as witness the smithies, inns and horse-troughs on other routes.

While Barnet was a coaching town, its own horses also consumed a lot of hay and produced a lot of manure. Farmers giving evidence to parliamentary select committees in support of a railway in 1845-6 complained that there were now only 40 coach horses kept at Barnet and that they had therefore to commute expensively to Smithfield, and looked forward to loading their horses, drivers and hay-laden carts into railway trucks towards London and receiving them back again manure-laden. The MPs were less than happy about the manure, but by 1853 the *Illustrated London News* was describing coal trucks which had brought market garden produce to the capital from 50-60 miles away, carrying on the return trip 'at a very low rate, the fresh stable manure from London – an item of traffic as yet in its infancy, but which is rapidly gaining ground'.

HAYMAKING

For much of the year the hay crop required little attention beyond manuring, but harvesting was very labour-intensive, and needed a massive inflow of seasonal labourers. Many of these came from Ireland, as well as from other parts of the mainland, and each year their situation was on a knife edge. They were only paid for actual work and there was no social security, so that if bad weather delayed the harvesting they very soon faced starvation. In 1830 it rained for three weeks in June, and a public subscription was eventually

52. Haymaking at Old Fold, from a map of 1726.

organised. John Trotter of Dyrham Park took the lead (as often), and on the 20th he distributed 730 lb (around 350 kg) of bacon divided into 2,400 pieces, while the innkeepers of the Red Lion and the Woolpack distributed 276 large loaves. The weather improved on the 24th and relief was discontinued, but the haymakers, who numbered 1,933 men and over 400 women and children, had not yet been paid, and a 'desperate riot' ensued, involving pitchforks and knives, and requiring over 200 people to quell it.

The harvesters' lives ensured that many were less than law-abiding, but there was also considerable prejudice. In May 1747 some Irish labourers sleeping rough at Kitts End held up a coach travelling from St Albans to the Green Man in Barnet so that they could raise the money to travel home; they had found neither work nor lodging, the latter 'because they said I was an Irishman and would not let me have any'.

A nonconformist missionary working in the area in the mid-19th century betrayed some similar prejudices, but also preserves a detailed picture of the harvesters' wretched conditions, even when the weather was kind:

> 'the Irish at this time of the year are to be seen in groups by the road side, or lying on the hay in the barns, these poor fellows are sometimes a whole month without changing their clothes, or even stripping, but lie down just as they return from the field...the little villages around, the lodging houses in Barnet and the barns of the farmers present an unusual influx of the Irish. The lodging houses in particular present a most disgusting and disorderly sight, especially on the Sabbath morning. It is not unusual to find 20 individuals, men, women, and children in one room, the women brawling, children crying, and the men laughing or swearing, some cooking, others eating while others are engaged in shaving or washing. As you go along the lanes of an evening you will invariably find near each farm house by the hedge side a fire of sticks and three uprights from which is suspended a pot, the poor haymakers are to be seen near the spot. Here the missionary can approach and will be allowed to read and to speak more plainly and faithfully than he dare in their native land – tracts are kindly received and a seeming attention is paid to the reading of the scriptures'.

On a happier note, Billie Olney remembered pre-1914 childhood games in the hayfields, taking care to leave no litter and carefully respreading the hay with sticks afterwards: 'We would build hay houses, magnificent affairs, rather like roofless

53. A haycart and other horse-drawn carts in Barnet High Street c.1900.

igloos, and play families in them, eat our picnics, and dive for cover when the lookout shouted "Farmer"'.

DAIRYING

By then, although Barnet was still separate from London, local agriculture was changing to meet suburban needs, and many farms went over to dairying. Billie Olney recalled her visits to Cox's Dairy at the junction of Manor Road and Mays Lane, where 'The walls were covered in cream and green tiles with pictures on them. The milk or cream was ladled out into your jug from large

54. Cox's Dairy in the early 20th century, with accompanying hens.

containers.' Dairy farms cooperated, so that the dairy at Elm Farm in Galley Lane bought in milk from Sharpe's Farm at Underhill and from Manor (Cox's) Farm if its own cows produced too little for its milk round.

PIGS

Pigs were better than other livestock at surviving by foraging in woods, and were the medieval peasant's mainstay. The animals' size, shape and requirements were significantly altered during the Agricultural Revolution, but as late as the 1870s children at East Barnet National School were regularly absent in October because they were collecting acorns for the local farms. As part of East Barnet's war effort a municipal piggery was opened near Cat Hill in May 1918, for which 450 residents had agreed to contribute their household waste, enough to feed twelve breeding sows. The enterprise lasted two years, and when it was sold as a going concern the *Municipal Journal* noted 'it is believed to be the only one which, after not only producing food during a critical period, is also able to show a profit at the close…'.

The scheme had been masterminded by Councillor Frusher, from 1900-39 a pig farmer at Folly Farm (on the south-eastern edge of Hadley Wood), many of whose animals were sent to London from

55. *The cows of Earl's Dairy at Hadley Farm walked through Hadley Highstone each day for milking. The herd was sold off in 1937.*

56. *A delivery cart from one of the area's many early 20th-century dairies.*

57. *The municipal piggery at Cat Hill, 1918.*

58. *The picturesque group of buildings at Folly Farm.*

John Radcliffe Esqr

Apr 1763 to Thos Emmerton £ s d

50 Small Scotch firrs at 6 each - 1 - 5 - 0
25 Lg Weymouth pines at 2 each 2 - 10 - 0
40 Larch firrs at 6d - - - - - 1 - 0 - 0
20 Lealooks in sort at 3d - - - - 0 - 5 - 0
12 Weeping Willows at 3d - - - - 0 - 3 - 0
20 Small mountaine arsh at 4d - 0 - 6 - 8
15 Duch Honeysuckels at 4d - - - 0 - 5 - 0
5 Monthley Roses at 4d - - - - 0 - 1 - 8
3 Damask Do - - - - - - - - - 0 - 1 - 0
2 Red Beljick Roses - - - - - - 0 - 1 - 0
2 Blush Hundred Leav Roses - 0 - 1 - 0
2 Double Velvet Roses - - - - - 0 - 1 - 0
1 Rose of Monday - - - - - - - 0 - 0 - 6
5 Large Double Matts - - - - - 0 - 5 - 10

Received Septembr 16th 1763 £ 6 - 6 - 0
the full contents of this Bill
and all demands
by me Thos Emmerton

59. John Radcliffe's account with Emmerton's nursery, 1763.

New Barnet station. He also kept a butcher's shop in East Barnet Road, and in summer the family diversified further, turning Folly Farm into a pleasure resort. Children came from across north and east London on Sunday School outings and school treats, and there was a small fairground, as well as famous teas. On one day in the year the station master appealed to local residents for flowers for the East End children, each of whom returned home with a bouquet 'from the country'. In the First World War Folly Farm was also used both for military parades and for the peace celebrations.

NURSERIES AND MARKET GARDENS

The ancestors of today's garden centres developed from the 17th century, and by the 18th were divided between nurseries, which grew and sold living plants, and market gardens, which sold produce. Barnet and Hadley were well placed in relation both to the aristocratic London market and to the various gentry seats, and with greenhouses and fertilisers able to overcome the local soil, became in the 18th century a significant nursery centre. The relationship with the upper classes, with both parties interested in collecting and developing new species, and involved to some extent in both plants and produce, crops up again on page 116.

60. The mulberry tree surviving in Queen Elizabeth School's playground, c.1930 (see p.50).

Thomas Emmerton established a nursery in a field on Mimms Side in 1729, and his sons expanded northwards (the first of several expansions and alterations) with another field whose southern edge is still marked by Nursery Row. The nursery specialised in the trees which were so essential for gentlemen's parks, but Isaac Emmerton III (d.1823) was also famously the author of the *Plain and Practical Treatise on the Culture and Management of the Auricula*. He must have found Barnet particularly convenient for one of his key compost ingredients: pigeon dung steeped in animal blood from the butchers. The happily-named William Cutbush, whose family had a nursery in Highgate, took over the Emmerton nursery around 1840, and it remained Cutbush's until closure, specialising in stove and greenhouse plants, shrubs, roses, fruit trees, bulbs and seeds. Utilising the family name, topiary too was a speciality. The original field was sold to become the barracks site *c.*1859, and the Territorial Drill Hall was built on the St Albans Road (Nursery Row) site in 1937, precipitating a closing down sale which included 25 greenhouses.

Other nurseries included Henry Clark's, from 1767-1783 next to the original Emmerton site, and Cornwell's. The latter had land near the physic well in 1817, and a field leased from Harrow School on Wood Street immediately east of Queen Elizabeth School. When the school expanded across Harrow's field in the 1870s, one mulberry tree was spared, which graced the playground for the next half century. Warwick Nursery, latterly Easton's, which specialised in flowers, started in the late 19th century with grounds first at the Highstone and latterly at Grimsdyke Crescent, and a florist's shop in Barnet High Street.

London's insatiable demand for fruit and vegetables was met by market gardens. There were plenty of these in the surrounding areas, though surprisingly few actually within Barnet and Hadley. Barnet Market, though, probably also attracted smallholders' surpluses, although how much this continued in the reconstituted market of the later 19th century, which concentrated far more exclusively on cattle auctions, is unclear. The *Illustrated London News* description of the Great Northern mainline in 1853, referred to above, while stressing that consumption was still 'infinitely below the wishes of the population', noted that 'Vegetables can now be brought by rail from fifty to sixty miles off in as short a time, and in as fresh condition, as by market cart from Barnet, Finchley, Greenwich, Hampton, or any place within eight to twelve miles of London'.

61. *One of the Warwick Nursery glasshouses, east of the Highstone and perilously close to the boys' hockey game. This glasshouse was replaced by a house, Eldenhope, in 1914.*

'The better inhabitants...'

'From Tudor times at least' wrote Cass in his *History of Hadley* ' the better inhabitants of Hadley were mainly drawn, as at the present day [1880] is still the case, from the professional and mercantile classes of the metropolis', and he went on to lament that the resulting constant changes of ownership and occupation made tracing the tenurial histories of the various houses extremely laborious. Cass was still part of an historical tradition, and world view, which unquestioningly limited local history to such families and their houses. Today the tendency is to focus more or less entirely on what used to be termed the lower orders, which corrects the balance, but taken too far distorts the more hierarchical past of which Cass is entirely representative. The point is important in this area because for centuries it contained a disproportionate number of wealthy families. The concentration of Georgian mansions in Hadley still bears witness to this, and Oak Hill and Osidge are survivors of an equally notable number in East Barnet. This concentration was not simply of architectural significance, but influenced all aspects of community life.

THE PEOPLE
The arrival of merchants started well before the Tudors. From at least the 13th century, when the Frowyk family of goldsmiths built a manor house at Old Fold, London's rich sought country estates within easy reach of the city, and from then on are to be found in ever increasing numbers in all districts within this sort of radius from the capital. They were attracted particularly to areas with good transport links, and to healthy gravel-topped plateaus such as Hadley. As the draw of London increased, merchants wanting rural retreats were joined by gentry and upwards whose main seats were elsewhere but who wanted another residence within commuting range. Many property transactions were also purely for investment: Henry Parker, citizen and painter-stainer of London, who acquired Little Grove in East Barnet in 1653, in his death-bed will of 1670 ordered his wife to sell it to pay debts incurred 'through the late Conflagration and other the Providences of God upon the Cittie [the Great Plague of 1665 and Fire of 1666] and my losses thereby'. Cass on occasion devotes pages to families whose activi-

62. *In the mid-15th century Henry Frowyk served as Lord Mayor of London.*

ties were centred elsewhere, but following him down those paths is unnecessary. He also garnered plenty of evidence for residents who played significant roles, whether nationally, locally or both, and who provide a series of snapshots which can be accumulated into a more general sense of local society. Previous success or the fortune of birth allowed a wider stage to such people, who in turn, in a world without television, radio or general literacy, brought a breath of outside events into the locality.

ROYAL VISITORS
Chipping Barnet lived with the continuous excitement of the main road, but the other areas were also sometimes involved. At her accession in 1558 Elizabeth I stayed at Hadley manor house on her journey from Hatfield to London, and in 1611 Lady Arabella Stuart (or Seymour) was detained locally. Inheritrix of a claim to the throne through her father, Arabella was seen as a threat by both Elizabeth and James I, and spent much of her life under virtual house arrest in various places. On the road in 1611, she stayed for sixteen days in an unspecified Barnet inn, where the costs included 30s (£1.50p) 'for glasses broken and in

63. *This portrait of Lady Arabella Stuart as a forceful-looking child hangs at Hardwick Hall, Derbyshire.*

rewardes to the meaner servauntes', and was then transferred to a house (either Church Hill House or Monkenfrith) in East Barnet. Here she stayed for 65 days, and the comings and goings, and logistics of supplying her establishment, must have made a considerable impact. The dietary allowance for herself, her servants and attendants came to a lavish 109s 4d per day; the stable accommodated three litter horses, one sumpter (pack-) horse, five coach horses, and a coach; and the rector earned £5 'for his paynes in attending the ladye Arabella Seymour to preache and reade prayers'. And if this was not memorable enough, Lady Arabella escaped by dressing as a cavalier over her petticoats and walking southwards down what is now Brunswick Park Road towards Betstile and awaiting horses. But she was recaptured at sea and thereafter imprisoned in the Tower until her death in 1615.

BLUE STOCKINGS

During the Gordon Riots, the violent mob mayhem which swept London in 1780, the Hon. Mrs Boscawen in nearby Colney Hatch (Friern Barnet) wrote to Mary Delany

'This country is full of *refugees*. Mrs. Chapone is at Mr. Burrows [the rector of Hadley], and I saw

64. *Hadley Rectory, seen beyond Latimer's Elm in the early 20th century, and obviously somewhat altered since the time it housed the Burrows family.*

her last night. Mr. and Mrs. Cole at Mr. J. Baker's at Enfield Chace Gate [Bohun Lodge], they fled on Wednesday night like Lot out of Sodom, the fire raining upon their heads. Dr. Munro's family are at Mrs. Smith's at Hadley, they fled from a friend's house, which was between two others that were burning, I am not sure where. We saw all this conflagration on Wednesday night from our garret windows....'

Frances Boscawen, Mary Delany and Hester Chapone, three of the relatively few women to feature in the original *Dictionary of National Biography*, were leading members of the Blue Stocking circle, a network of friends with similar interests which (contrary to modern assumptions) included male relatives, friends and mentors, among them Mr Burrows, Samuel Johnson and Samuel Richardson. Cass, talking of another member, Mary Sharpe (whose father had owned Little Grove and whose own country residence was South Lodge in Enfield Chase) is dismissive of 'a society of ladies and gentlemen who amused themselves with the assumption that they were somewhat in advance of their age', but in this he betrays his prejudice. All were indeed far in advance in believing that women were innately as intelligent as men, and in encouraging their writing and discussion of serious works of religion, philosophy and literature. Hester Chapone (1727-1801) published the highly successful *Letters on the Improvement of the Mind*, reprinted at least sixteen times in the 18th century and a further fifteen in the 19th.

The richer members of the circle, and particularly Elizabeth Montagu, also provided London with its *salon* equivalents, and within a group which set so high a store on friendship, warmth and common sense as well as wit and style were essential. Hester Chapone became friendly with the Miss Burrows, John's three sisters, around 1758, and from 1770, when he became rector of Hadley, she was a frequent visitor there. In 1762 she wrote to Elizabeth Carter (Johnson's colleague and the translator of Epictetus) 'How much am I, and how much are the Miss Burrowses obliged to you, for the very valuable and delightful acquisition you have made for us in Mrs Montagu's acquaintance', and a decade or so later, writing from Hadley, described being invited along with Amy Burrows to Mrs Boscawen's to meet the Abbé Reynal, who produced 'an unceasing torrent of wit and stories...as much as would have made him an

agreeable companion for a week, had he allowed time for answers.... Mrs Boscawen is a very good neighbour to us here, and a most delightful companion everywhere'.

John Burrows educated Mrs Montagu's nephew; was praised by Mary Delany (she of the exquisite paper collages of flowers) as 'a man of true Christian principles, as well as of learning and superior genius'; and detested the 'intolerable cold' of Hadley, where he nevertheless continued until his death in 1786. Sadly, a set of bereavements deprived Mrs Chapone of most of her family as well as many of her friends, and her mental and physical health failed. Her surviving friends helped with a move to Hadley in 1800, primarily to be near Amy Burrows. She died on Christmas Day 1801 and is buried in Hadley churchyard. Fanny Burney, the most famous of the younger generation of blue stockings, lamented 'How is our Blue Club cut up! But Sir William Pepys told me it was dead while living; all such society as that we formerly belonged to, and enjoyed, being positively over'. In fact the group (though not the friendships) had altered by the mid-1770s into something grander and more diffuse, but by the century's end the greater tensions induced by the French Revolution and the Evangelical revival had made its particular supportive networking style no longer viable.

OTHER AUTHORS

In similar vein, Juli[an]a Yonge, author of *Essays and Letters on the Most Important and Interesting Subjects*, *A Practical and Explanatory Commentary on the Bible*, and other works, moved into East Barnet manor house in 1778-9. Letitia Elizabeth Landon, the youthful poetess, lived at Trevor Park from 1809-15, although her writings, as Cass observed 'can scarcely be said to have stood the test of time'. The desire to claim more resonant names sometimes leads to point-stretching. William Makepeace Thackeray the novelist (1811-63) may have visited Hadley but only to see his mother, cousin, or the grandfather whose name he shared and who lived and was buried there. Anthony Trollope (1815-82), certainly visited Hadley regularly after his mother and sister moved into Grandon in 1836; the move could not halt his sister's TB, and Anthony draws on her burial in Hadley churchyard in *The Bertrams*. His mother Fanny, also a distinguished author, also drew on Hadley locations.

65. *John Hadley as Vice President of the Royal Society.*

OSIDGE

The way in which merchant money rapidly supported gentle (in the class sense) pursuits is beautifully illustrated at Osidge. In 1652 this estate was bought by George Hadley, a member of the London Grocers' Company; two generations later John Hadley, a Fellow of the Royal Society from 1717, played an important part in the development of the telescope, and himself invented the quadrant, still a familiar navigational aid to sailors. His brother George, also an FRS, was the first to formulate the correct explanation for trade winds. Much later, in the early 1890s, Osidge was bought by the rather more flamboyant Thomas Lipton, a Glaswegian self-made millionaire twice-over, first from developing a chain of grocery stores and then as a tea merchant. It remained his home until his death in 1932, with the house, its exotic servants and furnishings, the annual party there for the 500-odd London staff, his close friendship with Edward VII and, from 1898 until 1930, his repeated, unsuccessful, challenges for the Americas Cup, bringing him enormous fame and popularity. He bequeathed Osidge as a nurses' home, thus ensuring its survival.

66. *Sir Thomas Lipton's tree house at Osidge, c.1900.*

67. *David Livingstone.*

68. *Hester Chapone's house at Hadley, 1800-1, renamed Livingstone Cottage after David Livingstone stayed there in 1857-8.*

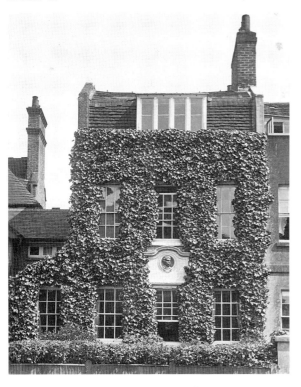

DAVID LIVINGSTONE

One of the best known local inhabitants is David Livingstone, even though he stayed a bare nine months. Nevertheless his first leave from Africa, spent with his family at what is now Livingstone Cottage (previously Hester Chapone's retreat), was significant. He produced *Missionary Travels and Researches in South Africa*, his four children played hide and seek in Hadley Woods, and Livingstone later wrote 'We spent no pleasanter time in England than the months in Hadley'. He attended the Congregational church in Wood Street, but also struck up friendships with the vicars of Hadley and of Christ Church Barnet.

THE ESTABLISHMENT

Cherry-picking tends to overlook the solid concentration of judges, physicians, soldiers and administrators of the Empire who were the main occupants of the great houses throughout the 18th and 19th centuries. The English taste for cluttering churches with memorials may be questionable, but they are a wonderful source of social history, regularly linking the private and public spheres. The Dury family memorial at Hadley commemorates not only Lt-Col. Alexander Dury, who bought what was thereafter known as Dury House in 1784, and did not die until 1843, aged 86, but also his wife, who died in 1805 aged 41; Thomas, the second son, who died in 1803 aged 15 of yellow fever while serving as a midshipman aboard *HMS Aeolus* on the Jamaica station; and Francis, the youngest son, a lieutenant in the 49th Regiment, who died in 1813 aged 17 of a wound received during the American War of 1812-15. Major-General Augustin Prevost (himself originally Swiss) survived his participation in the earlier War of American Independence. As interesting as his lengthy funeral monument is the entry in the East Barnet baptismal register for Christmas Day 1781: 'Pamela, a negro servant belonging to Major General Prevost of Greenhill Grove…was baptized in this Church by the name of Mary. The Sponsors were the Lady of General Prevost, Miss Juliana Yonge of East Barnet [the authoress mentioned above] as Proxy for Miss Mary Burton of Upper Brook Street Grosvenor Square, and the Rev. William Tait.'

INTERIOR DECORATION

Furnishings and gardens were an important aspect of what would now be called lifestyle, reflecting (as now) a mixture of individual taste and subservience to fashionable trends. Individuality fuelled the picture collections. In the 1760s Robert Udny, a London merchant who had acquired Bohun Lodge, formed a collection which afterwards passed to Catherine the Great of Russia; and in the same house George Knott (d.1844) collected the most distinguished contemporary English painters. In the interim, the Monro family of Beacon House were friends and patrons of the young Turner, who in 1793 made two watercolours of Hadley Church.

Wills and inventories sometimes illumine the furnishings. In his will of 1756 John Sharpe of Lincoln's Inn and Little Grove bequeathed his wife 'the use of all the household furniture in my said house at East Barnet of all kinds, woollen and linen, useful and ornamental, books, pictures, china, and everything else, with all brewing utensils etc., and also all the greenhouse plants etc, and also my wagons, carts, cart horses and saddle horses (except the horse with the side saddle and furniture, which my daughter usually rides on, which horse, etc. I give to my said daughter)...Item, I give to my wife both my coaches with my chariot and post chaise, with all my coach horses and the harnesses, etc.'

GARDENS

Gardens and grounds were very important. Francis Atkinson of Ludgrove acquired extra land for a bowling alley in the 1630s, and there was one at Church Hill House in 1703. More generally, gardening (or its supervision) became an ever-increasing passion from the 17th century onwards, both fuelled by and fuelling the development of specialist nurseries *(see also pp. 49-50)*. William Cattley (?-1832), merchant, eminent botanist, and 'one of the most ardent collectors of rare plants of his day' lived in Wood Street (on the site of the later Victoria Hospital), where he cultivated the first Corsage Orchid to reach these shores, subsequently classified as *Cattleya Labiata*. The biggest gardens also marketed greenhouse-

69. *A photograph of one of Turner's paintings of Hadley church, made when he was staying with the Monros at Beacon House.*

70. *A watercolour of Greenhill Grove, c.1820.*

grown fruit and vegetables. Michael Rochford was head gardener at Oak Hill in the 1850s-60s, taking over an establishment particularly famed for its pineapples and Black Hamburgh grapes, the latter regularly fetching 16s (80p) per pound at Covent Garden while others went for a mere 1s 6d (7.5p). But from the later 1860s conservatory-grown pineapples and peaches were losing out to imports, and Rochford decided to give up working at Oak Hill and concentrate instead on his own nursery at Enfield, which became a household name.

Gardening was also a sphere in which women could be involved: Mrs.Tempest of Little Grove spent a lot of her widowhood from 1794 to 1817 improving its gardens, plantations and pleasure grounds. Even so, the construction of a lake there was left to her successor. Most of these labour-intensive glories have vanished, although the Hadley gardens are still famous for their trees, there are remnants in some gardens at Cat Hill, and the Greenhill Grove lake survives.

THE HOUSES

East Barnet

The view from Church Hill Road across the steeply sloping parkland of the Pymmes Brook valley still gives some sense of the earlier ambience, but apart from Oakhill and Osidge the buildings have gone, leaving remarkably little reliable description. If the set of watercolours made in the 1790s and now at the Guildhall Library are to be be-

71. *Trevor Lodge on Church Hill Road, c.1880, when the house to which it was the lodge also survived (see p.58).*

lieved, the owners of country seats in East Barnet had all opted for pattern-book updating, creating a homogeneous array of rectangles ornamented with pillars, stucco and rustication.

Central East Barnet

The rebuilding process was continuous. Trevor Lodge, today an isolated and much altered survival, started life as the lodge for Trevor Hall, alias Church Hill House, designed in 1860 by Philip Webb and demolished in the 1930s. The Hall stood near an earlier Church Hill House, which had been bought by the Trevor family and demolished in the 1820s. This in turn had probably replaced the previous manor house. All stood nearer the church than the village, where the only large house was Dudmans, later known as the Clock House, which was there by 1619 when it was inhabited by Ralph Gill, the keeper of the lions at the Tower. It was demolished in 1925 but there are, for once, some photographs. Slightly east of the village was Little Grove, now marked only by a stretch of garden wall. There by the 16th century, it was rebuilt in 1719 and named New Place, but the older name quickly reasserted itself. It was greatly enlarged by Frederick Cass, father

of the local historian, who bought it in 1827, and among other alterations added a west wing and a lake, and demolished the chapel. His architect was John Buonarotti Papworth, and the plans survive in the RIBA archive. The house was demolished in 1932.

The Chase Edge

Buckskin Hall, known for part of the 19th century as Dacre Lodge, was within the minority portion of Cockfosters lying within Barnet. It may have been the 'messuage lately built near Sonnesgrove' referred to in a will of 1558, and its fresco shown in illustration 73 clearly celebrates the delights of the Chase in the early 17th century. It had been completely updated by *c*.1800 and was demolished around 1930. Also at Cockfosters, West Farm alias Norrysbury alias West Place belonged to the Norris family by the 1620s, but the surviving house was rebuilt *c*.1825. Southward, Mount Pleasant, latterly Belmont, also seems to have been built in the later 16th or early 17th century and then updated. It too was demolished *c*.1930.

Bohun Lodge, so-named by 1779, was really Bourn Lodge, or the house near Bourn Gate, the gate into the Chase at the top of Cat Hill. A house

72. *Clock House in the early 20th century. The clock from which it was named, clearly visible here, survives above Clockhouse Parade, the house's replacement.*

73. A 19th-century drawing of the fresco at Buckskin Hall.

was there by 1602, and in 1636 Richard Rea, gentleman, was allowed to lay pipes across the Chase to draw water to it 'provided always that he do not stop up the well, but it may lay open for people's use and for His Majesty's deer to come to the water to drink'. It was bequeathed along with neighbouring Oakhill as a theological college in 1928, but demolished in the 1950s.

74. Belmont (formerly Mount Pleasant) in the late 19th century, with its standard 18th-century rebuilding somewhat obscured by later accretions.

75. Oakhill, from an early 20th-century photograph.

Oakhill itself was 'lately erected' in December 1790 within the grounds of Monken Frith, which had been built by the 17th century and retained the area's medieval name, meaning monks' wood; it was demolished in 1937. Oakhill has been substantially remodelled: it gained its current east front between 1810-32, and has 20th-century additions. At the southern end of the Chase-edge string is Osidge, where there was a house by the 1650s which had gone by 1767. The surviving replacement, yellow brick with stucco trim, was new in 1808.

The Western Side
Lyonsdown and its estate were transformed into New Barnet in the mid-19th century; the house, certainly there by 1652, went in 1862, and is apparently unrecorded. Its southern neighbour, the medieval Pricklers (from the Prittle family; the name survives in Pricklers Hill) became known from the 16th century as Greenhill Grove or Park. It featured in the Stucco Patent Case of 1778 (in which John Liardet and the Adam brothers successfully challenged John Johnson's separate patent on 'a composition for covering the fronts and tops of houses and for ornamenting the same') as one of the houses to which Johnson had applied his stucco. General Prevost granted the southern part of Greenhill to a relative in 1782, who built a house there called Belle Vue. This was bought around 1820 by Thomas Wyatt, an East India merchant (and not to be confused with the architect of the same name and generation), who demolished and rebuilt, naming the new house Willenhall. Alterations in 1828-9 were again by the versatile Papworth (the son of another stuccoist) and the plans, listed as Pricklers Hill, are again at RIBA. Willenhall was demolished around 1900, and Greenhill in the late 1920s.

Hadley
The grand houses at Hadley have fared considerably better, although The Priory, next to the church and partly 16th-century (but entirely non-monastic), was demolished in 1958. The updating which produced the beautiful Georgian cluster helped ensure that very few pre-18th-century traces survive. The 13th-century moat which once

76. *The Priory at Hadley, never religious but with its sham-gothic frontage hiding an earlier building. Its demolition was inexcusable.*

77. *Sent in 1906, this card captures one of Hadley's groups of Georgian houses. Like many others it is wrongly titled, calling what is in fact the Green the Common.*

enclosed Old Fold manor house now encircles the 18th green of the golf course. Part of Hurst Cottage is 16th century, and Pymlicoe House, Beacon House, Hadley Lodge and The Chase all incorporate 17th-century elements. All parts of the 18th and early 19th centuries, though, are well represented, and Pevsner wrote in 1953 that 'The combination of Hadley Green and Hadley Common results in one of the most felicitous pictures of Georgian visual planning which the neighbourhood of London has to offer.... Of the houses... only a few are of high individual merit. It is their universally satisfying standard and their variety of scale, texture, and juxtaposition that makes them so enjoyable.' He also noted that Hadley's charm is 'elusive to the descriptive word', making the best course to head there armed with Pevsner (the revised edition, *London 4 North*, is fuller, if heavier) or Gelder, and explore.

CHANGE

By the later 19th century even Hadley was no longer attracting top-level new housing, and although there are substantial late Victorian and Edwardian mansions, notably at the Hadley

Common end of New Barnet and at Arkley, they are not in the same league. The seriously rich were seeking other areas, but the political and social changes of the 20th century, loss of Empire, reform of the inheritance laws, wider access to the professions and so on, in any case largely ended the sort of society portrayed above. Largely, but not entirely. On the whole, the Georgian houses at Hadley were not preserved by conversion to institutional use, and some of their residents have maintained the high tradition. Kingsley Amis and his wife Elizabeth Jane Howard lived at Lemmons from 1968-76. Robert Carr, Conservative Foreign Secretary, lived at Monkenholt from 1954-1981/2, and was ennobled in 1976 as Lord Carr of Hadley. (Reginald Maudling, Chipping Barnet's MP from 1950-79 and holder of many of the high offices of state, was a carpet-bagger.) One truly extraordinary survival is Wrotham Park, still today operating as the Byng family's full-scale country house, but although it owns Old Fold and casts a quasi-feudal shadow over Hadley, it lies just beyond our area.

Looking after the Poor

Widespread poverty has always been the human norm, and Britain's welfare state and national health service, creations of the 1940s (combined with compulsory education since 1870), have so radically changed the situation that it is often easier to recognise our past in societies which have not yet been able to follow suit. For Roman Catholics, as for the followers of most other religions, charitable works are an essential part of salvation, and although most such activities are undocumented, bequests to the poor feature in wills, both in the middle ages and later. Nevertheless at the Reformation Protestant theology introduced a harder-nosed distinction between the deserving and undeserving poor, which discouraged indiscriminate alms-giving. Unfortunately the distinction was and remains easier in theory than in practice, and was also formulated at a time when economic dislocation was causing many casualties.

POOR LAW ACTS
The Poor Law Act of 1601 made parishes responsible for poor relief and empowered their churchwardens and overseers of the poor (the latter a new office) to levy poor rates. The money was to be shared between relief of the unsupported sick and old, setting the able-bodied to work, and putting children whose parents could not support them into apprenticeship. Until the Poor Law Amendment Act of 1834, which combined parishes into larger unions, coping with poor relief became every parish's predominant concern. The Act of Settlement of 1662 gave the overseers the right to remove any newcomer likely to become a charge on the parish, and appalling amounts of time, money and human misery were expended in repelling and removing outsiders. Current responses to asylum seekers are strikingly close.

REMOVALS
Local records detail removals both far and near. Chipping Barnet parish in 1688 appealed successfully to the magistrates against accepting Elizabeth Dell from Gaddesden, since her previous settlement had been in Mimms Side, and its extraditions included Mary Sandforth, whose husband had abandoned her and her three chil-

dren there in 1771, but whose settlement, and therefore his family's, was at Kingsbury.

Barnet and Hadley were also caught in the slipstream of London's social ills. A constant stream of homeless people, termed vagrants, came along the Great North Road, and the overseers either paid them small sums to move on – Barnet made 429 such payments in nine months in 1742-3 – or paid fees to have them escorted on their way. Wider morality died, as witness payments in 1738 'to a man that had smallpox to go forward, 1s' and 'to sundry sick people to goe on, 1s 1d'. Numerous entries about 'getting a great bellied woman out of town' reflect the danger of possible settlement by birth, but also the predicament of London serving girls seduced and then thrown out by their masters. Similarly runaway apprentices were often escaping inhuman treatment. It was an indictable offence to harbour vagrants, in case they gained settlement, and John Nix of Barnet was so indicted in 1769.

APPRENTICESHIPS
Many of the poor were children, and when they were old enough most, like Henry Palmer, apprenticed in 1721 to 'Master Joseph Tufnell, Barber and Periwigg maker, at the upper end of Old Street', were sent to London to gain both a trade and another settlement. The overseers tried to ensure the children's well-being, but many masters saw them as an expendable source of cheap labour and the Barnet entry for 1716: 'For horse and self going to attend ye Justices…about James Hodges girl being starved by her master', is far from unique. Some apprentices too were less than ideal: William Brunt, a Barnet currier, complained in 1835 that Benjamin Harrison had absented himself without leave and indulged in drunkenness and abusive language, and the contract was discharged. Unusually, it had also included the service of Harrison's eldest son, showing that the father must have been older than most apprentices, and that his family's misery was set to continue.

OUT-RELIEF
In communities where everyone knew everyone, payments to the old and sick were usually well directed, and the system was far from heartless. Nevertheless poverty and private dignity could hardly co-exist. In 1691 Henry Smith's gift of £20 per annum to Barnet was used to provide 'coates with a badge on them' to 'the aged poor, infirm people, and married persons having more children in lawful wedlock than their labours can

maintain'. These provided much-needed warmth, but identified the wearer as a pauper – and one prohibited from begging – and were therefore unpopular. All recipients of Hadley parish alms were badged in 1721.

WORKHOUSES
Cost-cutting and belief in the deterrence principle always played their part, particularly in the workhouses. Chipping Barnet had its own workhouse from 1729; Hadley was using a cottage near the pound as a poor house by 1731, fitted up a better building in 1738, and moved into the former foundling hospital at Hadley *(see p. 108)* in 1768. East Barnet too was using a pair of cottages as a workhouse, probably from the 1730s. At Hadley the dietary allowance was increased by half in 1776 after complaints that it had been severely cut, and from 1799 the male inmates had to wear yellow stockings and the women blue uniforms. In 1836 Ann Gray was admitted to Chipping Barnet workhouse to await examination by a magistrate 'for selling her Union clothing'.

Both the 18th-century Agricultural Revolution and the Napoleonic Wars caused great economic dislocation and a surge in the numbers of the poor. By 1821, Hadley Vestry was sure that 'the increasing pauperism which distinguishes the present day, is chiefly attributable to the absence of the Honest Pride, which once characterised the British Peasantry, who would suffer every hardship rather than apply for parochial assistance. This first principle being depraved, he steps into poverty and crime, for they are now almost synonymous terms...and should the present state of insubordination continue, the consequences are too dreadful to contemplate'. Its solution was to establish a tread mill so that paupers could, extremely laboriously, grind grain for a payment 'sufficient to support existence'. This, they hoped, 'by giving employment to those who really desire it will be a great means of restoring the deserving man to his place in society...and also discover the imposter who only makes the want of an employment an excuse to starve his wife and children'. The other, unstated, hope was that it would deter workhouse applicants.

Neither this nor other would-be treatments of the effects rather than the causes had any likelihood of success. In a more fundamental attempt to solve at least some of the problems, the Poor Law Amendment Act of 1834 ordered that parishes be combined into Poor Law Unions, administered by Boards of Guardians. This ended the

78. *These cottages at East Barnet, demolished in the 1930s, are similar to those in which the parish workhouse was placed.*

business of settlement. The section of Hadley Highstone which was still included within Enfield parish *(see p. 12)* became part of Edmonton Union, but the rest of our area joined Barnet Union, which covered ten still predominantly rural parishes. Its guardians first met on 6 July 1835, to discover that although they had inherited five workhouses, even Chipping Barnet, the best and rebuilt at considerable cost in 1807, was badly arranged and could only hold forty inmates. Land on Barnet Common was therefore purchased for a new workhouse capable of holding 150-200 people, and the paupers were transferred in spring 1837. The chance survival of the Workhouse Master's diary from 1836-8 gives glimpses both sides of the transfer, showing how the workhouses helped transients as well as long-term inmates. In June 1837 the Master noted 'an Irish Casualty Woman and her infant who was delivered a few hours before in a Ditch at East Barnet', and the following April another Irish woman was admitted with two children and 'an infant female 19 months old in her arms quite dead'.

More cheerfully, in March 1838 the rector of Hadley sent 'a quantity of Toys and Dolls...for the use of the Boys and Girls', and in December

1837 'The inmates had all plenty of Roast Beef and Plum Pudding on Christmas Day and was very comfortable except the Cook who got intoxicated soon after Dinner. We sent her to Bed.' Much later, to celebrate Queen Victoria's jubilee all the men were given beer and tobacco, the women new petticoats and the children toys and sweets, and all were then taken to see the decorations in Barnet High Street.

Workhouse conditions were intended to act as a disincentive, with the Act prescribing tightly limited rations, but this was virtually impossible since the inmates were at least assured of food, clothes, bedding, and sick care. During the cholera outbreaks in Hadley and South Mimms in 1854, one of Captain Trotter's missionaries recorded 'At Hadley, where were many deaths...in some houses not a blanket could be found'. The disincentives were therefore the dehumanising rules. Although Barnet was reckoned a liberal workhouse, its regulations classified the inmates into seven categories separated by age and sex, which meant that elderly couples and families were entirely split. Only clergy were allowed to visit without permission.

The workhouse closed in 1939 but its infirmary wing continued as a hospital, the core of the

79. Barnet High Street as the group from the workhouse would have seen it. These decorations are celebrating either Victoria's jubilee in 1897 or Edward VII's coronation in 1902.

80. A ward in the workhouse infirmary, probably in the early 20th century.

current Barnet General *(see p. 108)*. Family memories of the workhouse recorded in the local *Times* in 2000 included a grandmother's fear of going into Barnet Hospital and dying there because 'she had grown up with the stigma of that place being a workhouse before it became a hospital'. Other memories, though, showed the gap in the safety net left by its closure. One woman recalled that she and her brother were put there when their mother had to go into hospital, and a former resident of Union Street (so-named because it led to the Union workhouse) remembered the tramps 'coming up the road to the workhouse. I used to see them at around 4pm every day. They would stay at the workhouse overnight'.

ALMSHOUSES

Private charity was always an important part of poor relief, a point made obvious locally in the remarkably large number of almshouses. Most have a similar pattern of an original endowment enhanced by later bequests, and of periodic enlargement and modernisation.

Hadley

Sir Roger Wilbraham, of Clerkenwell and Ludgrove, built his almshouses for six poor women in 1612. In 1678 another lawyer, Justinian Pagitt, conveyed the old vicarage house in trust to provide residences for the rector, parish clerk and six poor couples or single women. From 1788

81. The charmingly Gothic Pagitt's almshouses at Hadley.

two of the almshouses were leased to the rector to pay for the repair of the rest, but even this was not enough, and after some £200 had been raised, four new houses were built in Gothic style *c.*1822 on an adjoining part of the rectory garden; two more were added in 1848. The charity remained underendowed, and in 1984 was taken over by the Jesus Hospital Visitors.

Chipping Barnet

The earliest endowment was Eleanor Palmer's, a bequest of 1585 of two acres of meadow in Kentish Town to the use of the poor of Chipping Barnet and Kentish Town (two-thirds to Barnet) for ever. This land, around today's Kentish Town fire station, produced modest rents as pasture until 1820, when builders were granted development leases, and soon afterwards, in 1823, the Barnet trustees were able to build six almshouses in Wood Street. Two more were added alongside the renovation of 1930, and a further 22 off Chesterfield Road in 1984-5.

The earliest actual almshouses were built by James Ravenscroft, lawyer and merchant, and known locally as the Great Benefactor. James bought land in Wood Street and built six

82. The Jesus Hospital Charity.

almshouses, as their plaque records, in 1672. A detailed set of regulations and permanent endowment in the shape of a small piece of land in Wood Street and a substantial ten acres in Stepney followed in 1679, establishing what he chose to name the Jesus Hospital Charity on a solid basis. Once again 19th-century development increased the value of the Stepney land, enabling the Visitors to improve conditions in their own, Pagitt's, Palmer's and Garrett's almshouses, extend support to the Victoria Cottage Hospital and Queen Elizabeth School, and, at last, to build more almshouses in Potters Lane in 1929 and Grasvenor Avenue in 1934. There have also been subsequent additions.

Last of the Wood Street cluster are Garrett's almshouses, deriving from John Garrett's bequest of £800 in 1728. Garrett was widely generous, making other bequests including £100 to a fund for Dissenting ministers' widows, and £25 in trust to have 'five poor boys born of sober and honest parents' in Chipping Barnet bound apprentices, but the houses were underendowed and were taken over by the Jesus Charity in 1949.

Less well known are the Thomas Watson Homes in Leecroft Road, built in 1913-4 as its plaque says 'as a memorial to Thomas Watson by his daughters Annie and Florence for the benefit of old and loyal employees of Messrs. Sutton and Co., Carriers, with which firm he was associated for 50 years'.

Wealth made in the City and land purchased elsewhere as endowment were important factors for several of Barnet's almshouses, but in some cases the City link is directly obvious. The Leathersellers' Company bought land north of Wood Street in 1603, which was then let as pasture for over 200 years: the last leaseholder was John Knightley, a Barnet cow-keeper. In the 1830s the Company decided to add to its stock of almshouses and chose the Barnet site, and as Richard Thornton, the then Master, was laying the foundation stone in 1837, he asked to pay the full cost. The Company gratefully named the row Thornton's Almshouses, and he also paid half the bill for the facing row built in 1850-1. Adjacent land was bought on which the gatehouse was built in 1859-61, and a third, northern block followed in 1866 to house the inmates of the Company's almshouses built in the 16th century on the St Helen's Priory site at Bishopsgate. The splendid iron gates from St Helen's followed in 1926. Sympathetically modernised and rebuilt in 1964-6, the three blocks and their Gothick chapel (also of 1926) add greatly to the gaiety of Barnet's architecture.

83. An early photograph of the Leathersellers' almshouses.

East Barnet

Links with London were equally direct in the case of the Clock and Watchmakers' Asylum, built at the extreme southern tip of East Barnet. Fundraising began in 1853, land 'beautifully situated at Colney Hatch' was purchased, and the foundation stone laid in June 1857. Appeals continued, including the surprisingly modern insistence that the asylum was to provide a retreat for 'aged men or women of the trade, irrespective of all question of country or religious opinion….. The Christian and the Hebrew, the workmen of London or any other town in the United Kingdom, or even of America, may become occupants…and side by side pass their declining days. No feeling of exclusiveness actuates the promoters of this work'.

Two City Companies, the Goldsmiths and the Clockmakers, began to make annual donations, and in 1864 William Rowlands, a gold watchcase maker from Clerkenwell and one of the leading lights in establishing the almshouses, gave £1000. The first distribution of interest took place on 27 August 'on which occasion a handsome entertainment was given by the aforesaid benevolent donor to the friends of the Institution, including the inmates, in the grounds of the Asylum'. Further appeals allowed more houses to be built from the

84. The Clock and Watchmakers' Company was one of many bodies wishing to commemorate the royal jubilee with something of lasting public benefit.

85. Lancelot Hasluck, local benefactor and, from 1904-10, chairman of East Barnet UDC.

1870s onwards, and the whole site was entirely rebuilt in the late 1960s, reopening in 1971. Despite the potential for confusion with the more famous Colney Hatch asylum, the later Friern Hospital, the almshouses kept their original name until the 1920s, but by 1939 they had become the National Benevolent Society of Watch and Clockmakers' Homestead, and today are simply called The Homesteads.

The last in this considerable series of almshouses makes a fitting conclusion. Lancelot Hasluck, 1863-1937, who lived first at Greenhill Park and then at Arkley, devoted his life to local public affairs, serving on East Barnet Urban District Council and as a JP, governor of the Queen Elizabeth Schools, and trustee of various charities. In 1931 he conveyed six acres of built-up land in West Ham and Leyton to trustees, who when the leases fell in in 1946 were to purchase land in East Barnet for almshouses. In the event, with East Barnet being developed at a rate of knots, Mr Hasluck pre-empted himself and bought three acres of the Eversley estate, just south of Oakhill Park, in 1934, although the first houses were not put up until 1950-1.

MUTUAL AID

In distant kinship with medieval guilds such as the Holy Trinity at Chipping Barnet, mutual aid associations flourished particularly in the 19th and early 20th centuries. Because their rules and regulations had to be confirmed by the justices of the peace, we know of two Societies of Good Fellowship meeting respectively at the Bull in Barnet in 1806 and the Cat at East Barnet in 1807, of the Inner Society in 1821, also at the Bull, and of the Barnet Union Society at the Woolpack, formed in 1832 for the 'mutual relief of its members afflicted with sickness, lameness, blindness, or any such calamity, by which they are deprived of the means of supporting themselves and their families'. Some similar-sounding societies, though, notably the Barnet Amicable *(see pp. 116-7)* were purely social clubs.

86. The Cat at East Barnet, where a Society of Good Fellowship met in 1807.

Religious Life

Until well into the 20th century religion was central to the lives of individuals and communities. In the middle ages the Church had the monopoly of education, and priests and monks provided virtually all the country's administrative, educational and welfare services. Rather than receiving salaries, they were supported via landed endowments. Barnet was one of St Albans Abbey's many manors, and Hadley belonged to Walden Abbey – hence the prefix Monken.

Local government was organised on a parish basis from the 16th-century Reformation until the late 19th century. The Reformation did not alter the monarch's divine role, which meant that religion was not simply a matter of private belief but also an important public test of political loyalty. The law requiring weekly Anglican church attendance was not repealed until 1836, but was not enforced after 1689, when the Act of Toleration included registered nonconformist places of worship. The civil disabilities of refusing to subscribe to the Acts of Supremacy, exclusion from the universities and all Establishment professions and offices, remained very real until the 19th century.

THE CHURCHES
St Mary, East Barnet and St John, Chipping Barnet

There was certainly a church within Barnet by 1157, when it was listed in a papal bull confirming various St Albans possessions. This was the mother church, St Mary, which still contains Romanesque fabric dated to *c*.1140. Stretching the endowment was never welcome to incumbents and, however large the area, supplementary churches were seldom supplied within a manor or parish until the 19th century. Chipping Barnet, though, was a special case, and St John's had been built by Michaelmas 1276, when a court roll entry refers to an obstruction on the road leading to 'the church of Barnet and the market'. Nevertheless it did not become a separate parish church until 1866.

In 1435 the parishioners at Chipping were given permission to appoint and pay a priest provided the rector of East Barnet's income was unaffected, but this proved a heavy commitment, and in 1449 they were allowed to found the Guild or Chantry of the Holy Trinity *(see p. 30)*, whose members formed a corporation able to hold property in common from which to support a chaplain. Soon afterwards the church was rebuilt, primarily at the expense of John Beauchamp of Barnet; the

87. St Mary East Barnet with its weatherboarded tower in 1795.

88. The plaque to John Beauchamp, who paid for the mid 15th-century rebuilding of St John's.

plaque requesting prayers for his soul, though relocated and partially defaced, still survives.

The guild chaplain cannot have provided a complete solution, and services in both churches must have been suffering, since in 1471 the abbot of St Albans effected a settlement of the 'diverse strifes, dissencions, and debates'. In future, 'consideringe that in Chepinge Barnett is more

89. The plaque with the date 1494 over the door at St Mary's Hadley.

and greater number of people, and alsoe more recorse of strangers then is in East Barnet', the parson was to perform all the services at St John's 'in his owne person or by a deputie' and all the services at St Mary's in his own person. From then until 1866 the rector remained at East Barnet and there was a curate at St John's.

St Mary, Hadley

The first reference to any religious establishment at Hadley comes *c.*1140, when Geoffrey de Mandeville granted a hermitage within his park there to Walden Abbey (Essex). By 1144 there was a religious community, presumably an expansion of the hermitage, and by *c.*1175 a parochial church. The current building bears the date 1494 over the door, but this is from the rebuilding, the 'reparacions and bielding' which were still continuing in 1506. The new building probably overlay the old one, but is less likely to have been on the hermitage site. Certainly by the 17th century it was outside the park. There was also a mortuary chapel, built after the Battle of Barnet in 1471, whose location has never been identified.

ALTERATIONS

Rebuilding and enlarging occurred across the centuries, as did radical internal transformations in line with changing liturgical practices. The most drastic change occurred at the Reformation, when along with the dissolution of monasteries and chantries, walls were whitewashed and many furnishings and vestments swept away. In later centuries galleries and pews accrued, while in the 19th century enlargements and 'restoration' often amounted to virtual rebuilding.

East Barnet's chancel was rebuilt in 1632, and a wooden turret at the west end was distinctly post-medieval. This was briefly replaced by an octagonal belfry, and then in 1828 by the present tower. Cass noted that 'This unpleasant construction absorbed, it is believed, the larger part of subscriptions destined to the general improvement of the edifice'. While cash was still short G. E. Street (later the architect of the Law Courts in the Strand) undertook some minor alterations in 1849 and uncovered a medieval piscina and some patterned wall painting. The church also retains some fragments of 13th-century glass. A south aisle was added in 1868, and the chancel lengthened in 1880.

Street had already been active at Hadley, where in 1848-9 he widened the aisles outwards and removed two galleries. William Butterfield,

90. *The interior of St Mary's Hadley recorded just before the alterations in 1848.*

91. Butterfield's enlargement of St John's, with its bright external chequerwork, has ensured its continuing domination of Barnet Hill. This view, taken in the 1950s, features both a trolleybus and a bus.

always a more aggressive architect, effectively rebuilt St John's in 1871-5, keeping the 1453 nave and north aisle but adding another, higher nave and south aisle, and replacing the west tower.

BELIEF AND THE BEGINNINGS OF DISSENT
Even in the middle ages belief was never uniform. There are plenty of wills reflecting real piety: bequests to the fabric of the three churches, to their many altars and lights, 'a pelowe of selke' for the high altar at St John's, and so on, as well as payments for funerals and requiem masses. Nevertheless there was also considerable dissent, and, strengthened by direct experience of repressive ecclesiastical overlords *(see pp. 29-30)*, it is no surprise that heresy found local adherents.

LOLLARDRY
The Lollards, who were heavily implicated in the Peasants' Revolt of 1381, denied that the existing social hierarchy was God-given ('When Adam delved and Eve span who was then the gentleman?'), and insisted that the Bible ought to be available to all in English, rather than restricted

to Latin and priestly mediation. In 1427 William Redhead of Barnet was forced publicly to abjure doctrines learned from the vicar of Totteridge and to burn his pernicious, presumably Lollard, tract, and in 1470 Margaret Lucas of Barnet was excommunicated, again most probably for Lollardry.

THE REFORMATION
Attitudes to the Reformation were highly mixed. The general right of access to the Bible passed from heresy to orthodoxy, and was probably widely welcomed. There were probably also few local tears at the dissolution of St Albans and Walden abbeys in 1538, but the destruction of a whole structure of life and belief, and the suppression of much that offered both spiritual and aesthetic consolation, was far from universally welcomed. The ending of the Holy Trinity Guild in 1547 with the dissolution of the chantries was probably particularly unpopular.

The Reformation's ultimate success was not due to popular feeling, helpless either way against brutal Tudor power, but to the shortness of Queen Mary's reign, from 1553-8. Had she lived as long as her sister and successor Elizabeth, her resti-

92. *The cross in the foreground of this picture, painted c.1800 by S. Peake, may commemorate the place of William Hale's martyrdom. Local tradition puts this both in Church Passage (which was slightly further south before the churchyard extension) and at the junction with today's Park Road. A closely similar picture has joints of meat hanging in the windows of the corner butcher's shop.*

tution of Catholicism would almost certainly have succeeded. Nevertheless, the vast and rapid sale of monastic and chantry lands, creating a stake in the Reformation for the purchasers, was hard to reverse, and the accompanying terror, though no different from that already inflicted for the Protestant cause, also served to repress rather than convert. The only known martyrdom at Barnet was that of the Protestant William Hale, in 1555. Henry Machyn's diary recorded: 'The xxxi day of August whent out of Nugatt [Newgate] a man of Essex unto Barnett for herese, by the shreyff of Medyllsex, to borne [burn] ther', but he fails to explain why Barnet was chosen. Latimer's Elm, which stood on Hadley Common until 1935, was popularly supposed to have been named after Bishop Hugh Latimer of Worcester, also martyred in 1555, but was in fact probably named from a local 17th-century resident.

LATER DISSENT

While religion was used to legitimise the social and political hierarchy, tolerance was impossible. As James I put it, No Bishop equals No King. Queen Elizabeth was a reluctant zealot, unwill-

93. *Latimer's Elm, distinctly the worse for wear after a storm in March 1916.*

ing 'to pry into men's souls', but the Acts of Uniformity and Supremacy passed in 1559 placed very high penalties on public dissent. Catholicism was again proscribed, but despite the risk a few locals held out: in Hadley Ralph Noble was indicted for recusancy in 1582, as was Anne Berrowe in 1640, and there were said to be three papists in the parish in 1676 and one in 1706.

Protestant dissenters of various hues, all those who agreed with Robert Browne (the founder of Congregationalism, 1550-1633), that the church should not be governed by state, monarch or bishop, were equally unhappy with the Elizabethan settlement, and the first Stuart kings' insistence on their divine right to unfettered rule, and resultant Civil War, did nothing to soften attitudes. Many radical Anglican ministers were ejected, including Ely Turner, removed from Hadley in 1644 and still not replaced five years later. (Also in 1644, the Quaker George Fox re-

corded 'I went into Barnet....Now during the time that I was at Barnet, a strong temptation to despair came upon me, ...and sometimes I kept myself retired in my chamber, and often walked solitary in the Chace there to wait upon the Lord'.) Charles II was personally tolerant, but his restoration in 1660 did little to heal the breach, and the Third Act of Uniformity in 1662 ensured a further wave of ejections.

THE INDEPENDENT CONGREGATION IN CHIPPING BARNET

Among these was Samuel Shaw, the minister of St John's, ejected in 1662, who responded by setting up a meeting (religious group) in his own house. In 1669 Richard Baxter, the eminent preacher, who was living at Totteridge, wrote that 'this market town of Barnet ... which had been extremely addicted to the Conformist way... now is so much altered that though the town

94. *The Independent (later Congregational) chapel in Wood Street as rebuilt in 1824. Part of the graveyard of the previous chapel is still visible from Union Street.*

consists of so much of inns and alehouses, which are very seldom Nonconformist, a private meeting near the church is crowded like as the churches were, and the church is almost empty'. Whether the meeting had survived since Shaw's day is uncertain, but its drawing power was now due to John Faldo, who had begun a ministry 'in a room in a common yard in Wood Street', regarded as the direct ancestor of today's United Reform church in Wood Street.

Faldo, a rigid Presbyterian with what the historian of the Wood Street church has called 'the religious narrowness which does little to commend the Christian gospel', wrote the vitriolic *Quakerism no Christianity* while at Barnet, and the more tolerant Baxter, who preached there, found the congregation averse to all forms of singing. In the early 18th century, when the minister may have become too intellectual, not to say heretical, for his flock, membership dwindled until in 1732 the church folded. Nevertheless Celia Fiennes,

noted local resident and travel-writer *(see p. 37)*, gave £1 a year for ten years in her will of 1738 (proved in 1741), adding to her previous gifts of a table cloth and pewter plate for Communion. Hopefully all were used when the congregation re-emerged for a decade in 1748; but it failed to survive the sensational ministry of Thomas Marryat, who appeared in the pulpit in bright robes, was less than teetotal, and eventually ran away abandoning his wife and children.

Another start was made in 1797, but the group of avowedly Calvinistic dissenters, confessing 'our guilt helpless and deservedly wretched state as sinners', attracted few adherents. Alexander Smith, the minister who from 1821 took his congregation into the mainstream, later recorded

'There I found Dissent not only at a discount – hated by the church folks, suspected by the tradespeople, but fair game for the pelting of the rabble. There I found the old chapel little

95. The still current United Reform (previously Congregational) chapel which replaced the 1824 one in 1893. This photograph was taken before 1907, when the adjacent cottages were replaced by the church's Ewen Hall.

better than a hovel, concealed from public view by surrounding objects, as if ashamed of its existence. That town I left with a neat little chapel...with a good frontage...Dissent respected – our position recognised – our countenance courted – my ministry at Bible meetings, Infant School meetings, on a par with clergymen, while my connection with the young men of the town and the Mechanics' Institute placed me above them in the general estimate of the town'.

Splits were not entirely a thing of the past – there was another in 1873 when a minister was considered too Anglican – but from then on the Congregational church had a respected role in the town's life.

OTHER EARLY GROUPS
The Wood Street meeting has the longest history but there were other groups, although most or all of the seventeen dissenters registered in Hadley in 1676 probably attended Wood Street. Samuel Hodges of South Mimms, a Quaker already fined for holding a 'seditious conventicle' in his house, sold land for a meeting house to William Wyld of Chipping Barnet in 1686; the site was at the southern end of Potters Bar, but attracted members from further south. A group which had previously met in a house at Kitts End joined it

c.1707, but the meeting faded from the 1770s. Methodists established a meeting in two cottages at the Hadley end of the High Street in 1760, and John Wesley preached there in 1777, recording mournfully 'Will this poor barren wilderness at length bloom like a rose?' The cottages were replaced in 1839 by the chapel (now Baptist) which still stands. Until the Baptists bought the building, in 1891, other sects had failed to flourish in Hadley: William Lloyd registered the schoolroom of his house for Independent worship in 1808, but two years later there were only two dissenters in the parish apart from Methodists, and no Independent chapel was established.

ROMAN CATHOLICISM
The 1689 Act of Toleration did not extend to Roman Catholics, and the very mild extension of their rights in 1780 precipitated the Gordon Riots in London, and the flight to local safe-havens of various wealthy non-Catholics *(see pp. 52-3)*. An Act in 1791 allowed chapels and schools to be built, but Catholics remained debarred from teaching in endowed schools, and when the Headmaster at Queen Elizabeth's School converted in 1837 he had to resign. A mission from Kentish Town eventually established a chapel in a room in Union Street in 1849, bravely enough since Barnet was apparently known at the time as 'one of the most bigoted places near London'. Nevertheless when

96. *A picture taken c.1880 of the original Methodist chapel at the Hadley end of Barnet High Street. It was sold to the Baptists in 1891, with whom it continues.*

97. The Lady Altar in the enlarged church of Mary Immaculate and St Gregory, Chipping Barnet, in the early 20th century. This church burnt down in 1973 and has been replaced with a set-back building in angular modern style.

the solitary priest got stuck abroad by the Franco-Prussian War in 1859 the mission nearly closed, and in 1860 he was having to serve both Barnet and Waltham Cross. At the end of the year, though, Father Bamfield was appointed at the head of a larger establishment; he stayed at Barnet until his death in 1900, and under him the church was enlarged, a school 'for boys of the middle and poorer classes' started in 1868, and a community of priests, the Institute of St Andrew, founded in Wood Street, with responsibility for both Barnet and Bushey. The community had folded by 1914, when its premises were taken over by the Sisters of St Martha for their convent and school.

THE CHURCH OF ENGLAND

In 1804 the Nonconformist Wood Street congregation had founded Barnet's first Sunday School, whose success in the 1820s led the outraged Anglicans to thunder biblically 'let the Dissenters beware of thrusting their sickle into our harvest'. To which the minister superbly replied 'we first occupied the field, cleared the ground, and long gathered the first fruits'.

This was a typical spat, since the Church of England was beginning to stir, realising that its failure to react to the consequences of the Industrial Revolution, particularly the population increase and shift, meant that increasing numbers of souls, if reached at all, were reached by non-conformists. Part of the response was a bitter split between the High and Low factions, the former at the Roman Catholic and the latter at the non-conformist end of the spectrum. It was faction rather than population pressure which led to the first new Anglican churches in Barnet since the Reformation, when donors funded two low-church alternatives to St John's. St Peter's at Arkley opened in 1840 'to accommodate' (in the words of the 1851 Ecclesiastical Census) 'a few scattered and very poor people', and Christ Church, no distance from St John's but in Mimms Side, began as a chapel of ease of St Giles, South Mimms in 1845.

Christ Church was mainly funded by Captain Trotter of Dyrham Park, himself an active missionary and aid worker, and also the sponsor of missionaries whose activities at Barnet Fair and among itinerant haymakers are described elsewhere *(pp. 24-5; 45)*. In William Pennefather, the Irishman who became the church's incumbent from 1852-64, he found the ideal colleague. Among many other initiatives, Pennefather established the annual conferences which became the Mildmay Mission *(see also p. 109)*; placed orphans of Crimean War soldiers locally *(see also p. 114)*; and gave practical help to many of those affected by Chipping Barnet's loss of prosperity *(p. 32)*. The church hall which bears his name was

98. St Peter's Arkley, from a drawing by Charles Rea, c.1950.

99. *The spire of Christ Church visible beyond Pennefather Hall.*

opened in 1907. Christ Church, Cockfosters (or Trent), which opened in 1839, was and remains within Enfield, but its ecclesiastical parish continued to include the Hadley Highstone enclave until 1922 (although civil control was transferred earlier *(see p.12)*.

New Anglican churches finally began to be built routinely in new centres of population, and the old immense parishes were split. Holy Trinity Lyonsdown opened for New Barnet in 1864 and St Stephen's, Bell's Hill in 1896 next to the 1895 cemetery. St Stephen's was partly funded from the surplus of the Chancel Fund, James Ravenscroft's other great bequest to Barnet. As well as endowing the almshouses *(see p. 66)*, in his will of 1680 James also left land at Stepney to support the maintenance of his father's tomb (still the most magnificent monument in St John's), with any surplus to be used for church repair. Again as with the almshouse endowment, the rise in the land value in the 19th century generated a surplus which allowed the original aims to be extended. There were also temporary mission churches, including one at Duck's Island on Mays Lane.

100. *Thomas Ravenscroft's monument in St John's, drawn c.1820.*

LATER NONCONFORMITY

More numerous were the new nonconformist chapels which also sprang up to serve the enhanced population. In the Edwardian heyday choirs from the mainstream sects, the New Barnet Baptist, Wesleyan Methodist, Presbyterian and Congregational, and High Barnet Wesleyan Methodist and Congregational churches, all competed at the annual Barnet District Industrial Exhibition *(see p. 118)*. There was also a range of other groups. The buildings were many and large, often replacing initial temporary arrangements. As with the Anglicans, there were some principal benefactors: 'The handsome Weslyan Chapel which adorns the principal thoroughfare [of New Barnet] owes its erection very largely to Mr Morgan Harvey's generosity'. T.Morgan Harvey JP, of Bohun Lodge, had 'also given a drinking fountain and cattle troughs'.

THE SALVATION ARMY

The Salvation Army, more usually associated with inner city areas, had a strong local presence. The *War Cry* reported in August 1883 'High Barnet Grand opening. In the afternoon a lot of young men came with the object of making a row, but we fired some red-hot truth into them, and they were soon stopped. Place so much stirred that we thought it wise to have no open-airs. At night, good order.' Judging from the street directories, this was in fact at New Barnet, where there is still a barracks. The *War Cry* for 15 January 1887 reported from High Barnet: 'During the few weeks this place has been opened we have seen souls saved from sin and the devil', and this must mark the start of the meeting there, whose citadel opened in 1891. The movement's founder, 'General' William Booth (1829-1912), lived in Hadley Wood, and he and his family were greatly involved with the High Barnet meeting.

One of Barnet's few 19th-century black residents was a member: Daniel Allen, known locally as Old Dan the Negro, but in fact only 50 when he collapsed in 1891 while working, as he had for the previous decade, at Messrs Warren & Co's coal depot near High Barnet station. The *Barnet Press* reported that

'The local contingent of the Salvation Army (of which poor Dan was an earnest member) assembled …and a short service [was] held outside the Barracks, at which the orderly behaviour of the large concourse gathered to witness the spectacle, testified to the respect in which the deceased was held. The coffin, upon which were placed the hat and tunic of the deceased comrade, was deposited on a gun carriage covered with flags. The cortège was led by the Army band, and included a large number of followers, and the rank and file of the Barnet Corps of the Army. The Hymn "Sweeping through the streets of the New Jerusalem" was alternately played by the band, and sung by the mourners, on the route to the [Baptist] graveyard at Potters Bar'.

101. The Salvation Army holding an open-air meeting on the second day of Barnet Fair in September 1920.

DECLINE

The absolute centrality of religious belief is one of the most obvious ways in which the past was different. The reasons for the change are many and debatable, but high among them must come the discoveries of the early to mid-19th century which made it obvious to all but the most intransigent that the Biblical account of the Creation is inaccurate. With this fell the belief, previously shared by all sects (and still, whatever the Scripture, the mark of fundamentalists in all text-based religions), that the Bible was the literal and directly revealed Word of God, and thus the inescapable blueprint for all human activity. The danger that the whole edifice would crash was seen immediately, but in fact the consequences were slow to filter through, and other, less straightforwardly literal reasons for belief have of course remained persuasive.

Nevertheless, by the end of our period the change was obvious. Christ Church Barnet's centenary book, published in 1945, noted that during the war national days of prayer had filled the pews: 'But the contrast with ordinary Sundays was only too marked...the parish...has not escaped from the taint of prevailing spiritual coma which is so markedly manifest in our nation, in spite of all its appalling dangers and miraculous deliverances'. Looking forward, the book concluded: 'Our message has not changed, though old methods of proclaiming it may pass away. The need no longer exists for soup kitchens, coffee palaces, and continuation schools....Open-air services and parochial missions do not attract the crowds which once they did. The old methods may no longer serve us. Let us find new'.

In the half century or so since then, congregations have continued to dwindle, parishes and sects have merged, and overlarge buildings have bitten the dust. New Barnet has been particularly denuded: the Baptist chapel of 1872 went in 1982, and the Wesleyan Methodist and Congregational chapels, both opened in 1880, were pulled down in 1963 and 1967 respectively. The Salvation Army's High Barnet citadel closed in the mid-1980s. At the Hadley end of Barnet High Street, the chapel which the Baptists bought from the Methodists in 1891 continues, but the spires of the larger edifice slightly further south into which the Methodists moved have, since 1989, been part of the façade of the Spires shopping centre *(see illustration 5)*.

102. *Station Road, New Barnet c.1904, showing the pedimented Baptist chapel and the Congregational alternative with its Anglican-looking spire. Both have now vanished. Half visible in the foreground is East Barnet Town Hall, built in 1892 on a deliberately more impressive scale than Chipping Barnet's equivalent in Wood Street.*

Transport and growth

Transport and housing have always been linked, but not always in the same way. The early settlements in our area were strung out along main roads, but primarily in order to supply the needs of other travellers. The wealthy, the first to live here in some sense as commuters, did not travel into London on a daily basis, and anyway had their own horses and carriages. Despite coaches and omnibuses, daily commuting from this distance until rail and tram links existed would have been unusual.

THE MAINLINE
The London to Birmingham line, whose opening in 1838 spelled the end of coaching, ran west of our area. By 1845 three schemes were being touted involving Barnet. The proposed Eastern Counties' spur from Tottenham and the Barnet & North Metropolitan Junction Railway's plan for a line up through Hendon, both terminating at Barnet,

rapidly hit the buffers, but the London to York Railway Company obtained Parliamentary approval for its plans in 1846 and, by now named the Great Northern Railway Company (GNR), opened its line in 1850. Avoiding Barnet Hill, the line and Barnet station (renamed New Barnet in 1884) lay a mile and a half to the east. Privately run buses, particularly Parsloe's to Hadley, Clarke's to Arkley, and Bryant's to his inn, the Red Lion, helped bridge the gap. So too did the new Station Road and a well-used footpath, now Meadway. Mainlines were not particularly intended for commuter travel, but the company soon realised their potential, and another station was opened on the edge of the expanding suburb of Oakleigh Park in 1873.

THE NORTHERN LINE
The GNR was also developing suburban routes. In 1862 it became involved with the Edgware, Highgate & London Railway Company scheme for a line from Finsbury Circus through Muswell Hill to Finchley and thence northwards. The first branch, through Mill Hill East to Edgware (by then entirely GNR-owned), opened in 1867. The second, through Whetstone to Barnet, proved slower to arrive, and even when it finally opened

103. New Barnet railway station c.1900.

104. *The footpath (now Meadway) between the town of Chipping Barnet and New Barnet station, on a card sent in 1910.*

105. *Barnet High Street, with the Star Tavern facing Union Street, on a card posted in 1939. When a station site behind it was suggested, the tavern was having a spell as a coffee house. It was demolished in 1959.*

106. The Black Horse on Wood Street, near two of the proposed station sites. This card, which was posted in 1907 but may well be earlier, also shows part of the Leathersellers' Almshouses as well as a cattle trough and hay cart.

in 1872, the location of the terminus near the foot of the hill was a severe blow.

A decade earlier, in March 1862, a local committee had waited on the GNR to see if it would build a spur from its mainline, and had also decided that if possible the station should be sited at the back of the Star Coffee House 'for not only is it the most central that can be obtained for the town of Barnet itself, but it is best suited for the outlying districts...the inhabitants of Hadley could have no cause to complain; and for the residents upon Barnet-common and neighbourhood, a direct line of communication would be open to the station via Union Street'. The coffee house was almost opposite Union Street, and a plan was drawn up with a station rather lower, at the bottom of Moxon Street. The company opposed this and a projected spur by the Edgware Highgate & London; in 1864 it obtained parliamentary approval for a spur from its mainline to a station behind the Salisbury Arms, with a road down to an elevated Moxon Street, but then did nothing.

In 1866 once again three companies submitted rival schemes. The Midland proposed a station behind Moxon Street with a line proceeding through Friern, Finchley and Golders Green to Cricklewood. The GNR suggested a loop from the mainline, running south through Potters Bar, Barnet and Totteridge to join the Edgware, Highgate & London line near Finchley; Barnet's station would have been behind Christ Church, but in the face of protest this was altered to the south end of Barrack Field, near the Black Horse on Wood Street. The Edgware, Highgate & London proposed more or less the current High Barnet branch, but with a station west of the main road at Underhill.

It was this last which received parliamentary approval, but the company was promptly swallowed by the GNR, which proposed looping the line further west to a terminus (again) near the Black Horse. This was approved but two years of inactivity followed until, in 1869, the GNR won a two-year extension, and there were the first signs of action. By August 1870 almost all the purchasing was done, but only as far as the top, or 'close to the top', of Barnet Hill. The westward continuation to Barnet Common, apparently unprotected by contract, was dropped as too expensive and 'If the line is extended at all, of which Mr Oakley (the general manager) says there is not the least doubt, it will be continued across the fields to Hadley, and thence to Potters

107. *High Barnet station, nestling at the foot of Barnet Hill.*

Bar'. By May 1871 the *Barnet Press* reported 'The customary twigs with their scraps of paper attached, are now to be seen in the horse-fair field...giving an approximate idea of the site of the future station'.

The branch opened in 1872, and the station (despite its lowly position) was named High Barnet. Even in the 16th century the cartographer John Norden used High, instead of Chipping, Barnet but the name remained relatively uncommon until chosen by the railway. (Chipping, however, is now staging a comeback.) As part of the London Passenger Transport Board's rationalisations, the line was incorporated into the Northern Line via a new connecting tunnel to Archway in 1939, and the previous route to Finsbury Park discontinued. The track was also electrified up to East Finchley in 1939, and to High Barnet in 1940.

A FATALITY

Railway construction was dangerous, and in 1871 the Barnet branch claimed a victim. At the inquest his fellow navvies reported that Henry White, aged 23, was running his barrow along a plank when he slipped and fell fourteen feet, pulling both the plank and barrow down on top of himself. Many navvies were Irish, but White

was from Oxfordshire, and it an interesting insight into life before telephones, widespread literacy, or rapid transport that his father had neither seen him for four months nor known where he was working, but was contacted immediately the accident occurred. The *Barnet Press* noted that this was 'the first fatal accident which has happened during the six months the railway has been making, among between six and seven hundred men' and that all the funeral expenses 'were kindly paid by the contractor, Mr Smith; who said deceased was a very respectable and steady young man, and one of the best in his employ'.

NEW BARNET

The belief that railways always brought instant suburbia was and is unfounded, but there were significant connections. When the GNR was purchasing the land for its track in the 1840s, instead of limiting itself to the usual corridor, it bought the whole of the Lyonsdown estate which happened to be on the market (roughly the land between the early roads of Potters Lane to the north and Long Street, now Longmore Avenue to the south), took what was needed for the line and station, and immediately sold the rest to the British Land Company for development. The resulting suburb, New Barnet, previously

108. Part of the sale catalogue for New Barnet, published in January 1852.

simply part of East Barnet, grew slowly over the next half century, beginning with the main web of major routes, Station Road, Lyonsdown Road and East Barnet Road, and moving on to the infill. It was also extended northwards after the British Land Company added the Woodcock Farm estate, purchased in 1868. With areas nearer to London not yet full, New Barnet was far from a runaway success, but it remains an oddity, an island of Victorian and Edwardian housing surrounded by interwar development. It was also far less homogeneous than its later neighbours, with a deliberate range from cramped terraces east of the track to larger mansions further west and on the northern slopes near Hadley Common.

THE GREAT NORTHERN RAILWAY CEMETERY AND BRUNSWICK PARK

Hoping to capture some of the overflowing London market, the Great Northern Railway built a cemetery next to the track at Brunswick Park in 1861, complete with its own siding and coffin transfer arrangements. It was designed by Alexander Spurr and included one of London's finest cemetery chapels, since converted into a crematorium. The most prominent of the Victorian monuments is that for Shogi Effendi, leader of the Baha'i faith and grandson of its founder.

The cemetery survives, but the rail link was not a success. Even reducing the cost of hiring special funeral carriages from £1 to 10s (50p) was no help, and the sidings were closed in 1873.

As a result, 80 acres of the land were sold off in 1880, to become the suburb of Brunswick Park, our area's other surprising enclave of Victorian housing. The reason for the choice of name has never been established.

109. Although the name Tavern Hill has vanished, as has the Congregational church spire in the distance, this pre-1920 view westward past the Railway Tavern, at the heart of New Barnet, is still instantly recognisable.

110. *Looking northward up Lytton Road from Station Road, c.1900. E. Fergusson Taylor was a major local auctioneer and benefactor, and largely responsible for the imposing nature of East Barnet's town hall, which is just beyond the picture.*

111. *An illustration to a 1920s' brochure about the Great Northern London Cemetery. It is now called the New Southgate Cemetery and Crematorium.*

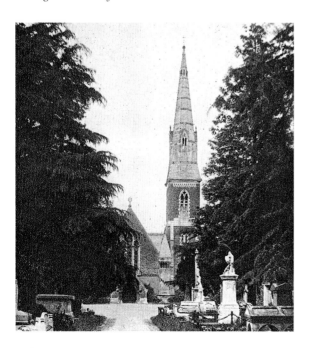

19th-CENTURY CHIPPING BARNET AND HADLEY

Situated at a road junction and plateau edge, Chipping Barnet's development was for centuries entirely ribbon-like, confined to Barnet Hill, the High Street and Wood Street. The first deepening began in the 1830s, just before the railways destroyed coaching, when Tapster and Moxon Streets were laid out on the east and Union Street (1837) put through on the west, the first stage in the fairly slow process of developing the arc between the High Street and Wood Street as far north as the still new St Albans Road. In the early to mid-century, following Barnet Common's 1815 enclosure, a number of new cottages were built around its edges along Mays Lane and Wood Street, and also at Hadley Highstone which, like the Hadley end of Barnet High Street, became an alternative and more populated focus to the old village centre.

None of these developments was related to the prospect of commuting, at least initially, and the stations' eventual locations were unhelpful. Manor Road, the first new road across the former common, was laid out from Wood Street down to Mays Lane in 1867, but by the 1890s neither

112. *Union Street in 1930, showing a row of original cottages, typical except for the assembly hall at no. 38. This started as a reading room c.1888, and among other uses served as a Pleasant Sunday Afternoon room and meeting hall (see p.89). It was demolished c.2000.*

113. *Some of the mid-19th-century cottages at Hadley Highstone. The ones seen here were in the enclave which remained part of Enfield until 1894, and had particular health and sanitation problems.*

114. *The southern end of Manor Road c.1900, still less than fully developed.*

this nor Bells Hill, a far earlier lane, was fully developed. Nevertheless development slowly gathered pace. North of Wood Street a sale catalogue was advertising plots in Salisbury, Carnarvon, Strafford, Alston and Stapylton Roads by 1881. Also around 1880 the Ravenscroft Park estate was developed slightly further west behind Wood Street; and the 1890s OS maps show similarly upmarket development beginning along Granville Road and Queens Road.

Union Street developed into something approaching a new town centre, with a significant concentration of churches and schools, a meeting room and, from 1889-1912, Barnet Town Hall.

REDUNDANT INNS, AND TEMPERANCE

Even the increasing population could not justify the concentration of inns along the High Street (although in fact across the whole area the number per head of population was on the low side), drink was seen as a major social problem, and the Balfour Act of 1904 allowed licence renewal to be challenged on the grounds of redundancy – an opening gladly seized by the Temperance movement. The Balfour Act was the basis of the 'Barnet comb-out' of 1927-8, which ended the Castle, Woolpack, White Horse, Queen's Head, Bulls Head, Hart's Horns and old Green Dragon in the High Street, and the Three Horseshoes and Queen's Arms at Underhill (although a successor to the last reopened on the opposite side of the road in 1937). Closures have continued, including the Wellington in 1964 and Salisbury Arms in 1988, and the Two Brewers at Hadley in 1992. The Cat at East Barnet was demolished after a fire in 1955.

As Richard Baxter noted in 1669 'the town [Barnet] consists of so much of inns and alehouses, which are very seldom Nonconformist', and since the antipathy was mutual, the area's strong 19th-century nonconformist presence ensured a strong temperance lobby. In 1909 H.E. Tidmarsh, the artist best known for his London street scenes, living in Marriott Road and (contrary to stereotype) a committed Methodist, called a meeting of 'the newly formed Barnet Temperance Council' at the PSA (Pleasant Sunday Afternoon, a nonconformist movement) Room in Union Street to consider the proposal that 'the temperance forces of the town, in order to do something more practical in combating the drink evil, should start a well equipped Coffee Tavern in a central position'; but the idea seems to have foundered. In 1928 the applicant for an off- licence noted that 'a new town had sprung up around the Bells Hill district – there being 600 to 700 houses in the locality – and the only means the inhabitants, who were generally of the respectable working class, had of obtaining intoxicating drinks was by going to public houses at the top of the Bells Hill or farther into town'. 264 people supported the claim but the objectors, predictably, were the licensees of the two pubs in alliance with the Temperance Council of the Christian Churches and the British Women's Temperance Association. Even the magistrates thought it odd that the temperance advocates preferred men to walk some distance to the pub, with the risk of a delayed return.

TRAMS AND TROLLEYBUSES

Succeeding where the railways had failed, the Metropolitan Electric Tramways line, which had reached Whetstone in 1905 and the county boundary on 4 August 1906, finally conquered Barnet Hill on 28 March 1907. The many postcards recording the opening day probably reflect real and widespread rejoicing. This terminus was at the top of the hill, just south of the church, and the line was never extended northwards.

Trams were at first known only by their individual car number, and those on the Highgate to Barnet route also carried the prominent letter B. Car numbers continued to be used, but other routes were soon added and route numbers appeared; by the end of 1913 route 38 ran from Highgate through North Finchley to Barnet and route 44 from Cricklewood through Golders Green and North Finchley to Barnet. Better and faster prototypes were also built, particularly car no 318, the 'Bluebell', which was built at Hendon and entered service in March 1927 (*see illustration 116*). Just three months later it ran into the back of a lorry halted by roadworks at the Underhill junction. The tram driver died, but the badly damaged car was rebuilt in a somewhat different form, and continued working until sent for scrap in 1936, when trams were being replaced by trolleybuses. The last tram from Barnet to North Finchley ran on 6 March 1938, with the same

115. The Queen's Arms on the eastern side of the road at Underhill. One of many with special provision for horses.

116. A tram standing at the Barnet terminus in the 1920s.

117. Drawing of the Metropolitan Electric Tramways car no 318, 'Bluebell'. From Barnet & Finchley Tramways, *by R.J. Harley (Middleton Press, 1997).*

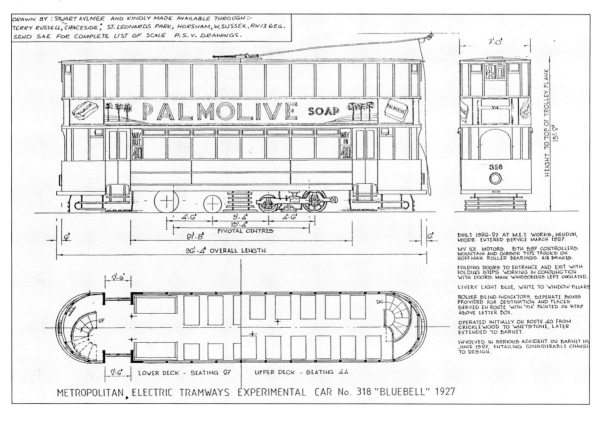

driver and conductor, W. Lowe and F. Mardell, who had taken the first tram up to Barnet in 1907.

Not only were the routes never extended northwards, but neither did any run east or west through Barnet – slightly surprisingly given the importance of New Barnet station. Thanks to the Tally Ho junction it was North Finchley which acquired eastward and westward connections and became an important hub, with the associated boost to shops and other leisure facilities. This situation continued with the trolleybuses: despite various route numbers, there was only the single spur up the Great North Road beyond North Finchley. The trolleybuses also continued to use the old tram terminus at Barnet, since the powers that had been obtained to build a loop via Wood Street, Union Street and the High Street were never used.

BUSES

Trolleybuses ended in 1961-2, when they were replaced by diesel buses, but buses, even if disconnected from stage coaches, have a longer history. A horse-drawn omnibus route linked Barnet and Finchley from 1898, but the first London & General Omnibus Company motor bus, plying from Golders Green through Finchley and Barnet to St Albans, started in 1912. Another route from Watford through Elstree to High Barnet followed in 1922.

In the 1920s private operators tried to fill some of the obvious local gaps. First on the scene was Charles Dunsford, proprietor of the Parkbridge Nurseries in Park Road, New Barnet, who, trading as Barnet Motor Services and with a garage in East Barnet Road, began running a bus from the Two Brewers at Hadley Highstone via Station Road to the Prince of Wales in East Barnet in 1923 (route 352), and another (route 354) also from the Two Brewers but to Whetstone and thence eastwards to Wood Green in 1924. Route 352 was extended northwards to Hadley Wood station in January 1925, and route 353 diverted from Wood Green to Totteridge and renumbered 354, but Dunsford ceased trading at the end of that year, the 352 ended with him, and the 353 less than a year later. The most successful private bus fleet was the Admiral, run by A.T. Bennett, which started further east on the pre-existing LGOC route 29, but pioneered an all-year round daily service northwards to Hadley Woods, previously only served at peak times for day trippers. All the bus companies were taken over by the new London Passenger Transport Board in 1933-4.

20th-CENTURY CHIPPING BARNET, ARKLEY AND HADLEY

The tram line ensured that the main thrust of Edwardian development was near Barnet Hill. The plots on Manor Road were finally sold, and the triangle between it and Barnet Hill speedily filled with Fitzjohn and Normandy Avenues and their neighbours. At the same time, and perhaps because of its seclusion, Arkley acquired a number of substantial detached houses.

The interwar years brought infilling. Meadway, previously the well-trodden footpath to Barnet Station, was developed from 1929; the Grasvenor Estate, built around 1932, filled the gap between Underhill and the Whetstone boundary; and new houses filled in the spaces at the lower ends of the roads that link Mays Lane and Wood Street. Moving outwards from the available transport links, the process would have doubtless have continued until Arkley and Hadley had become versions of East Barnet, but the war intervened in 1939, and the Green Belt was imposed thereafter. The Hadley Ridge estate, just north of Bath Place, is one of the few that straddles the war period. The interwar ribbon development along Barnet Road to Arkley has also continued, but there are still fields behind it, and genuine farms at the western ends of Mays Lane and Barnet Road.

There are plenty of examples of post-war housing, whether in small blocks of flats in and around Manor Road, brick and stuck-on timber executive closes at Arkley, or 1990s houses with mix and match architectural features of all periods and none at Hadley Highstone, but these have usually occurred through the piecemeal replacement of earlier buildings. At the upper end of the previous scale, large Victorian and Edwardian mansions requiring a permanent abundance of cheap domestic labour have been particularly vulnerable, and many of the flats and closes in Barnet and Arkley shelter behind earlier garden walls. At Hadley Highstone, in contrast, various small cottages have gone. Among these were some wooden ones at Mill Corner (part of the cholera-hit Enfield enclave of the mid-19th century), and Grocott Cottages just south-west of the Highstone. The latter were pulled down in 1958, although the scheme to replace them by Council housing was defeated by the newly (and specifically) formed residents' association. Common lodging houses too, both at Hadley and at Underhill, have vanished.

118. *A postcard of the newly-completed Fitzjohn Avenue.*

119. *(Above) Grocott Cottages at Hadley Highstone in 1958, shortly before their demolition.*

120 *(Top right) Jackson Road, part of East Barnet's extremely limited Victorian development. William Jackson, the road's builder, was unusual in being both licensee of the adjacent Prince of Wales pub and a leading local Methodist.*

121 *(Bottom right) Belmont Avenue and its surrounding streets are typically 1930s, although the road was still incomplete when this picture was taken in 1951.*

EAST BARNET

New Barnet apart, the 19th-century railways stimulated little development. Jackson and Capel Roads were laid out in the 1880s to link the village towards Oakleigh Park station, and a few houses were built in Oakhurst, Alverstone and Rosslyn Avenues in the opening years of the 20th century, but these remained exceptional. In the interwar years, though, when all the land nearer to London had been fully developed and East Barnet's turn was increasingly inevitable, the process was hastened by the extension of the Piccadilly line from Finsbury Park to Cockfosters in 1933, just east of the Barnet boundary but easily accessible. The population statistics tell the story: East Barnet Urban District (including New Barnet) contained 13,514 souls in 1921, 18,549 in 1931, and 34,480 in 1939. A Gallants Farm Estate catalogue of 1934 claimed that its 46 acres were 'the last undeveloped land within 10 miles of London', and described the 'comfortable farmhouse and homestead' which were, of course, doomed. Across the rest of East Barnet and Cockfosters the Greenhill Park and Belmont estates carried on the names of the mansions they replaced around 1930-1, with the Russell Lane estate following in the mid-decade. Rows of houses struck out across the hills

and dips of what must previously have been a spectacularly beautiful landscape. Although all the plans and designs were there, not all the estates were complete when building was stopped by the start of the Second World War in September 1939. Some houses are therefore post-war, but do not look it.

Private housing in the 1930s was cheaper relative to income than at any other period before or since, allowing a whole new swathe of society into its benefits. Changes in design also meant that the houses had better light levels, and often larger gardens, than their pre-1914 predecessors, but cheaper building processes and the concentration on a fairly narrow section of the market made interwar semis monotonous, and they were also extravagant in land use. For all their advantages, districts such as East Barnet lack the pleasures of architectural variety available in more slowly evolved areas.

COUNCIL HOUSING

Not all estates were private, and council housing too made a significant contribution, beginning when Barnet Urban District availed itself of the Housing of the Working Classes Act of 1890 to

122. A view of the newly-built Bevan estate, taken in 1951. This was again a delayed pre-war design.

build 22 houses in Barnet Lane in 1910 and 30 in Mays Lane in 1913. After the First World War, with Homes for Heroes conspicuously lacking, legislation and motivation improved. Between 1918-39 Barnet UD undertook seven schemes, of which the Chesterfield and Wellhouse Estate with 324 dwellings, and Grange estate with 110 were by far the largest. East Barnet UD embarked on its first two: 164 houses at Conyers Park, and at St Wilfrid's Road a slum clearance scheme of 30 houses and flats to replace some of New Barnet's worst jerrybuilding.

Again, some schemes were in storage during the war, and both councils continued to build after 1945. The only post-war developments with more than a hundred units were Barnet's Stanhope (193), Whitings Hill (431) and Little Larkins (115), and East Barnet's Bevan (130) and Cockfosters (419) estates. The London Borough of Barnet contributed the Dollis Valley estate on the former sewage farm site at Underhill in the late 1960s, before central government destroyed the system.

BREWERIES
There were plenty of alewives (and some men) brewing for sale in medieval Barnet, but larger-scale commercial breweries (where women scarcely feature) are rather later. Barnet Brewery operated intermittently in Wood Street from at least the 18th century until closure in 1909; council offices replaced it in 1912, leading Councillor Olney to remark 'Now a different kind of froth is produced on the site'. Another brewery, the Phoenix, was operating in Barnet High Street from at least 1866-86, but had vanished by 1896.

Hadley Brewery later claimed to have been founded in 1700, and in 1795 moved to a site at the northern end of Hadley Green. It was acquired in 1887 by J. Harris Browne, and rebuilt in 1890. Artesian wells beneath the brewery supplied the water for making ten bottled and ten casked beers, a pale ale and Hadley Stout. In the standard pattern, the brewery was sold to Fremlins in 1938 and brewing ceased although it continued to be used as a distribution centre; in 1967 it was sold again to Whitbread's, who ended its use entirely in 1969. It was demolished in 1978.

123. One of Hadley Brewery's delivery carts, with the obligatory dray horse.

124. *The frame assembly and wiring shop at STC, probably in the 1940s.*

FACTORIES
East and New Barnet: STC and Maws

The largest of the area's several factories was Standard Telephones and Cables (STC) which, as Western Electric, bought the first part of its site at the south-eastern corner of East Barnet (usually placed in New Southgate) in 1922. In January 1923 the first transatlantic radio telephone call was made from Long Island to a hut on the STC site, and until the 1960s the company remained at the forefront of international telephone and radio communication systems design and production. At its peak it was employing around 10,500 people, and was the archetypal 'family firm' (though not in the sense of family ownership). Women were always employed, although before the war only until they married. In providing an excellent range of sport and other leisure facilities, STC became a total way of life (there were many in-house marriages), and as they surged to and from the factory gates the workers were also the mainstay of many local shops.

Developments since the 1960s exactly mirror a wider revolution. Printed circuit boards (leading ultimately to the microchip) removed the need for mechanical systems and their labour-intensive production lines. Simultaneously, the British aerospace and telecommunications industries were decimated by America in the increasingly global market. STC suffered successive waves of redundancies, with the usual knock-on effects on local shops, while fewer and differently-trained staff, and a new management concern for cost-cutting, also weakened the old social side. The company was bought by Northern Telecom (Nortel) in 1990 and, according to a report of 1996 (by which time the employees had shrunk from the 10,500 peak to around 800), was reinventing itself as a 'systems company, changing from a hardware manufacturer to a leader and integrator of digital network solutions and services'.

Other local firms have also gone the way of takeover, usually followed sooner or later by closure. Maw's in Cromer Road opened in 1921, and made a wide variety of surgical dressings and pharmaceuticals until taken over by Johnson's and demolished in 1982.

CHIPPING BARNET

Despite these examples, the town of Chipping Barnet was the obvious focus for industry, and although its economy never recovered from being bypassed by the railways, from the later 19th century a certain number relocated there. A dental factory opened in Alston Road in 1891, now mainly remembered because its works team was one of those which later merged to become Barnet Football Club. Watson's, which started making high precision optical equipment in Clerkenwell in 1837 and moved to Holborn in 1860, opened a 'commodious factory in rural Barnet' (Bells Hill) in 1906. Particularly renowned for its microscopes, the firm also pioneered photographic and medical equipment, including in the 1950s the Barnet Ventilator, an electronic breathing machine developed in conjunction with Barnet Hospital, and the television zoom lens. After the family interest was sold in 1949, Watson's came via Pye to MEL, part of the Philips Group, and the Barnet factory closed *c*.1981.

PHOTOGRAPHY AND BIRT ACRES

Other firms with an interest in photography preceded Watson's to Barnet. Around 1880 John Swain's (which began as wood engravers in London in 1857, but rapidly expanded into newer print technologies) decided to establish a works in cleaner air away from the City. A house in Salisbury Road was purchased, followed by a site behind Bath Place, where surrounding cottages were gradually purchased and replaced by new factory buildings. Initially men travelled several times a day by train, carrying originals in (hopefully weather-proof) wooden boxes from the London office and works and returning with plates and proofs, but later two vans provided a daily service. Swain's was reunited in new premises at Clerkenwell in 1970.

At the southern end of the town, Hubert Elliott established Elliott & Son's photographic printing works in Park Road around 1890. With its Barnet Dry Plate Elliott's was one of the main producers of the gelatin dry plates which had since the 1870s revolutionised photography, and the firm also produced the *Barnet Book of Photography*, a manual which went through many editions and became a standard source. The introduction to the first edition, in 1898, claimed that 'In the mind of every photographer the name of Barnet is inseparable from the great Photographic Industry'.

That this is still true is no longer due to the manual, but to Elliot's recruitment as General

125. The entry to Swain's factory in the 1920s.

126. An advertisement for one of the many editions of Elliott and Sons' Barnet Book of Photography.

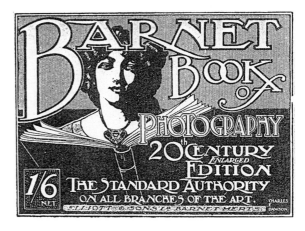

Manager in 1892 of Birt Acres (1854-1918). Acres moved into adjacent Clovelly Cottage (now 19 Park Road), until in 1895-6 he moved on, to found his own Northern Photographic Works, briefly in Salisbury Road but then in Nesbitts Alley off the High Street, and to live at Wrotham (now Manor) Cottage, Hadley Highstone. Acres was one of the most important pioneers of moving pictures. In May 1895 (the month of Lumière's first ever show in New York) Acres patented his Kineopticon camera, but already in March he had succeeded in taking Britain's first moving picture, the extremely short 'Incident at Clovelly Cottage' (to be viewed through an Edison Kinetoscope, not via projection). Another early success showed a hay cart crossing Hadley Green; as his wife and first audience, Annie, recorded 'It was short and it was jerky, but it seemed like a miracle'. On 10 January 1896 Acres gave Brit-

127. *This fundraising entertainment for St Stephen's
Bells Hill, advertised in the* Barnet Press *of 10 October
1896, included one of Birt Acres' early film shows.*

ain's first projected film show, to the Lyonsdown
Photographic Society of which he was a member. This therefore predates his first projected
show to a paying audience (sometimes hyped as
the start of commercial cinema in Britain) on 21
February. A supposed paying show in August
1895 at Barnet Town Hall in Union Street has
proved impossible to verify. Acres' main interests were the scientific and recording side of film-
making: his earliest films included part of the
1895 Derby and the opening of the Kiel Canal,
and he has been claimed as the founder of the
newsreel. On the technical side he collaborated
with R.W. Paul (who tended to monopolise the
credit), and he also left developing the purely
commercial and entertainment potential to others, including his assistant at Elliott's, Arthur
Melbourne-Cooper.

SHOPS

Permanent stalls and shops, particularly butchers', soon ringed the market place in Chipping
Barnet, where Church Passage was originally
known as Shop Row. Councillor Olney, born in
1860, remembered a butcher's shop 'with a porch
over the footway the whole length of the shop.
Formerly all the butcher's shops were so constructed' *(see illustration 92)*. He also recalled that
many of the shops had half doors so that 'One
could often see various craftsmen, such as cobblers,
tailors, and watchmakers, sitting…following their
various trades'. One of the most important
incomers was John James Cowing, who established his stationer's shop in the High Street in
1805. Two of his sons founded the *Barnet Press*
there in 1859, and Cowing's also produced an
invaluable range of local postcards and guides.
(Miss Gwynneth Cowing, among other activities
a stalwart of the Barnet Record Society, bought
Whalebones in Wood Street and replaced its
landmark bones.)

High Streets solidly dedicated to shops, like
department stores, were mid-late 19th-century
phenomena. Chipping Barnet duly followed the
trends, but modestly. It had William Stevens'
imposing drapers' store in the former Assembly
Rooms, but nothing to match Prior's at North
Finchley, and it was North Finchley's better transport links *(see p. 91)* that transformed it into the
more dynamic and expanding centre. Shops
outside towns were also sparse until the later
19th century, but then grew to a peak from which
there has been considerable decline. Hadley
Highstone, despite the nearby town, once had
two bakeries, two dairies, a butcher, fishmonger,
chandler, post office, confectioner, greengrocer,
builder and decorator, timber yard, and tea rooms,
and off-licence at the brewery. Arkley, smaller
but more remote, had a post office, store and tea
room. All have now gone: Hadley's last remaining village shop closed after the Barnet Waitrose
opened c.1960. Gone too are the local delivery
carts and vans. Around 1900 'in the East Barnet
Road alone over sixty horses and ponies were
owned and worked by bakers, butchers, contrac-
tors and fishmongers', and still in the 1940s there
was a delivery man 'driving an old horse-drawn
van, a long cart covered by a hooped canvas cover
seemingly painted with tar, like a less clean and
romantic prairie schooner'.

The spread of supermarkets, chain stores and
out of town shopping centres (locally at Brent
Cross) has now placed all high streets and indi-

128. *The slaughterhouse next to Shepherd's the butcher at 196 Barnet High Street, looking surreally festive c.1910.*

129. *Cowing's shop and printing office at 116-8 Barnet High Street, shown in one of the firm's many early 20th-century postcards.*

130. *The Welch family at their Sebright Road home c.1912. Well-known local coal merchants, they were descended from gypsies.*

vidual shops in peril. Chipping Barnet has been partly helped by The Spires development, opened in 1989, but has also suffered from some extremely dull rebuilding. Each generation will doubtless become nostalgic for the shops of its youth, but there are aspects to earlier memories which will not recur. One is the importance of the individual personalities who ran the shops. Edward Blishen (1920-96), the distinguished author, produced a litany of lament for the Barnet of his childhood: '...where is Friday, the butcher? Where are the Misses Goldfinch, and Vincent Papa, and Mrs Rock, who were all confectioners? Where is Mrs Channer, who ran the fancy repository? Gone are Jesse Smith, the baker, and Cicero Bennet, the cycle maker...'.

Another thread, before hygiene regulations and plastic packaging, is the engagement of all the senses: smell and touch as well as sight and sound (distracting muzak, however, is a recent invention). Sweet shops, serving sweets poured from glass jars into paper bags, always smelt inviting, while at Sainsbury's in Barnet High Street – as in every other grocer's – 'your cheese was cut with a wire, your butter shaped with wooden pats and the pattern put on it'. The written descriptions, good as they are, almost pale beside the wealth of surviving pictures.

131. *Manager Fred Dowling standing outside his branch of Robinson's (now closed), seen here in the 1930s. The other branch at Hadley has been joined by one in The Spires.*

132. *A row of shops at the Hadley end of Barnet High Street, on a card sent in 1908.*

Public services

Public services is a catch-all title for a whole range of provision that underpins daily life. Despite the range described here – policing, fire, sewage disposal, gas and electricity, health – everyone will be able to think of omissions. Some – education, poor relief, housing, cemeteries – can be found in other chapters, but the number is simply too vast to cover fully. There are some reasonable rules of thumb to help bridge the gaps. In earlier times the manor or parish was responsible for delivering most of the few statutory services, and local government has always continued to be a main provider. The range of services and providers moved sharply upwards in the later 19th and 20th centuries. Many facilities were highly local, so that the opening dates of primary schools (see next chapter), welfare clinics, branch libraries, parks and playing fields, are likely to coincide with housing development.

LAW AND ORDER

Barnet and Hadley are now leafy, relatively law-abiding suburbs, but were once far less tranquil. Crime was never confined to the town or to outsiders, but Chipping Barnet with its travellers, markets and fairs was particularly prone to disorder, and the situation was worsened by the area's location along the county boundary. The higher-level forces of law and order were county-based, so that a quick flight across the border (much practised by the fighting fraternity, *(see pp 121-2))* was often useful. A few examples are given of various types of crime.

ROBBERY

John Broade, a yeoman of East Barnet, stole a blue coat worth 2s.6d. from John Cooke at East Barnet in November 1589, but seems to have had a positive vendetta against John Smyth, also of East Barnet, gentleman. From him he stole a holland headsheet worth 10s (50p) and a double rail worth 8s, both on 4 January 1591; two days later he returned and made off with a sheet (26s. 8d), a yard-kerchief (4s. 4d) a currall (1s) a piece of woollen cloth (2s), a crimson satin hood (6s 8d) two silver whistles and a silver bell (2s); then, though by now a labourer of Hertford, he came back to remove a crimson hood (2s), silver whistle (1s) and coral (6d). The last time, surely oddly, he was found not guilty; after the 4 January episode, and to the modern mind equally oddly, he was one of the many who managed to exploit the loophole (a medieval leftover) that anyone who could read was a cleric and therefore not answerable in the civil courts. Two labourers, both from other areas, who respectively stole a brown cow (40s) and 27 sheep (£10) in 1589 and 1593 successfully pleaded likewise.

Highwaymen, the muggers of their day, targeted lonely commons. Crossing Finchley Common was therefore the main terror on the Great North Road, although there was the occasional incident at Hadley. Barnet Common too was dangerous: the Bishop of Sodor and Man was robbed in 1755 of 'upwards of twenty guineas by a highwayman masked and extremely well mounted', while in 1807 Sir David Baird was relieved of £100.

MURDER

In 1220 Alice Black confessed that she was present with her husband at the slaying of three men and a woman at Barnet, and was ordered to be burnt. In 1601 Alice Fulwood, wife of a barber in Chipping Barnet, was indicted for the murder of Mary Harwood, aged 16, by witchcraft. The local inquest had found that Alice was commonly thought to be a witch and had on several occasions bewitched Mary so that the back of her head was bruised, causing her death, but she was in fact found not guilty at the next Assize.

ASSAULT

In 1797 William Hoskin, a labourer discharged from the footguards as wounded and unfit for service, described how he was assaulted by Michael Walsh, the landlord of the Bull in Barnet, and flung out, only to be assaulted by several fishermen who carried him into the Market House and beat and kicked him there, also stealing clothing from his bundle and a tin box containing his discharge and one and a half guineas. (It would be interesting to know if the landlord was the same as the Michael Welch whose wife accused him in 1788 of assaulting her in the grounds of Green Grove near Chipping Barnet where he was then a gardener to the Duchess of Rutland.)

POLICING

Until 1840 there was a two-tier system of local law enforcement. At the local level was the manor, increasingly replaced from the 16th century by the parish. In areas like this where the manors

133. The stocks on Hadley Green, with Hadley Brewery clearly visible amidst the houses in the background.

remained strong, the handover was never absolute, and at Hadley particularly constables, headboroughs and beadles were appointed interchangeably. A man born in 1848 remembered the beadle: 'his uniform was a large blue coat with gold-coloured buttons; a wide, red collar edged with gold braid, and he carried a thick cane with a gold knob. He was a terror to us boys…'. Public punishment aimed to act as a deterrent, and Hadley bought a whipping post and cucking-stool in 1677. It also acquired new stocks in 1787, rebuilt in 1827 but reduced to a vestigial stump by 1935 when they were accidentally destroyed in the bonfire celebrating George V's jubilee. Hadley also had a pound for animals and a cage for humans. Barnet's lock-up was in Middle Row. The counties not only had courts and the justices of the peace, but also another layer of constables, particularly prominent during Barnet Fair *(see p. 26).*

THE BARNET ASSOCIATION

Policing in London was overhauled in 1792, but Barnet was way outside. Local associations were a standard response to law and order problems, and one was therefore formed the same year to cover Chipping and East Barnet. Its aim was the capture and conviction of offenders, and it was deemed so successful that in December its area was extended to cover Hadley, South Mimms and other adjacent parishes. The association's role, though, was limited to fund-raising and lobbying, and enforcement continued as before. Hadley, which had appointed paid watchmen in 1786, was doing so again in the 1820s.

THE MET

Robert Peel formed the Metropolitan Police in 1829, but Barnet was again outside and again responded by forming its own association, this time specifically to police the district. Two officers were engaged to patrol a limited area, later extended. Finally in 1840 the area was incorporated into the Metropolitan Police District.

Even this did not solve all problems. One of the nonconformist missionaries active at Barnet Fair

in 1854 noted: 'On more than one occasion we met with drunken policemen who were rushing about where accidents occurred more calculated to increase than prevent injury'. Sectarianism too stirred up conflict. According to the same, notably biased, source, when a drunken Roman Catholic attacked the missionaries and scattered their tracts, two policemen arrived, but were both Irish 'and immediately leaned to the Roman Catholic notwithstanding his violence. They said that we had no business to be there and if we did not go they would remove us. This is but a specimen of the folly of placing any confidence in any Roman Catholic in any official capacity when the question has anything to do with the state of their church'.

134. (Left) Barnet police station as built in the 1860s. Part of the forge demolished in 1909 to make room for the larger station can be seen on the left.

135. (Below) The same forge can be seen in this early photograph of Barnet Hill, taken in 1860 and showing the house which the first police station replaced. 'Tudor House' on the left was so-called from its style rather than its date. Note the absence of shops.

The site of Barnet's first police station is uncertain, though it was almost certainly in rented premises, possibly 85 High Street which was found at demolition to contain a cell door with a grille. In 1861 26 High Street was acquired, and a purpose-built station and section house constructed; then in 1909 28-32 High Street were also bought and demolished, and a new station built across the whole site around 1912. This was again rebuilt in 1974-6, and survives. East Barnet Police station was opened on the junction of Margaret and Edward Roads in 1884 and closed in 1933, although the building continued in other guises until demolition in 1985.

FIRE
In 1751 Chipping Barnet's leading residents started a subscription 'towards Purchasing a New Invented Fire Engine', and the next year proudly took delivery of the engine, 80 foot of pipe and a dozen leather buckets. The Local Board bought a Merryweather machine in 1868, and, moving on from another High Street location, the still-remembered station at the Hadley end was opened in 1890. East Barnet formed a volunteer brigade around 1870, housed at 3 Hope Villas, but went over to paid firemen and a proper fire station (at the junction of Lytton and Leicester Roads) in 1903. Fire brigades became increasingly professionally trained and equipped during the 1930s, providentially given their vital role during the Second World War. The formation of county-based brigades in 1948 led to the closure of the Barnet station, and the East Barnet one was replaced by the current premises on Station Road in 1991.

SEWAGE DISPOSAL
In the mid-19th century the connection between sewage contamination and the endemic outbreaks of cholera and typhoid was at last admitted, and in London work began on a system of sewers and distant outfalls. Barnet and Hadley were outside the metropolitan area but faced similar problems. New Barnet was developed from 1850, but its sewage was piped untreated into the Pymmes Brook, East Barnet's water-source. By 1868 there were three separate outbreaks of typhoid in East Barnet village, and 36 fever deaths. The parish vestry and its Sanitary Committee, after struggling for years against inadequate powers and resistant ratepayers, was finally able to construct

136. High Barnet fire brigade, in a card helpfully dated to March 1922.

137. *The new aeration tanks which helped update East Barnet's sewage farm in the 1930s. Some of the houses which necessitated the updating can be seen in the background.*

a sewage farm on land near Brunswick Road in 1871-2. This was also excellently run as an ordinary farm: 20,000 cabbages were immediately planted, and by the 1880s its oats and tares were also being sold at Barnet Market. East Barnet's population grew exponentially in the 1930s, the council installed a modernised disposal system to cope, and crop production had ceased by 1938. Chipping Barnet's sewage farm at Underhill, built from 1874 onwards, also grew crops but seems to be remembered primarily for its smell. Both farms became redundant with the installation of the Middlesex main drainage scheme in 1957.

The Hadley Highstone enclave within Enfield parish was notoriously unsanitary. In 1850 a preliminary report to the Enfield Board of Health on the whole of the parish's sewerage, drainage and water supply noted that some cottagers at Hadley Green had recently been subject to erysipelas, typhus and scarlet fever, which was attributed to defective drains. In 1854 the vicar of Christ Church Cockfosters, in whose parish the enclave still lay, wrote to the General Board of Health, pointing out that while most of Hadley 'is very elevated and generally very healthy. In a corner of this district there is an open Sewer

surrounded by a Population of nearly 100 souls. In this corner there have been 9 deaths from Cholera and at least 50 persons attacked by the disease in less than a fortnight; so much of the Sewer as is in Hadley parish is covered in [but] that part of it which is in Enfield is left open and is within 12 paces of the Cottages within which the greatest Mortality prevailed...', and complaining that his own complaints and those of the police to the Enfield Local Board had been ineffective. Enfield did in fact build a sewage works in 1855 and a larger sewage farm in 1877, but an 1878 report on Dury House suggests that Hadley was still having to make do with cesspits.

GAS, WATER AND ELECTRICITY
An East Barnet Gas and Water Company was incorporated in 1865, and had gas works in East Barnet by the following year, when its powers were extended. The company was licensed to supply gas to the whole of the parishes of Chipping Barnet, Totteridge, Enfield and Hadley, and parts of East and Friern Barnet and Finchley, and water to the parishes of East, Chipping and Friern Barnet, Hadley, Finchley and Totteridge. The

138. A Barnet Gas and Water Company lorry of the 1920s.

successor Barnet and District Gas and Water Company was incorporated in 1872. The main gas works were in Albert Road, New Barnet (closed in the mid-1990s), but other places feature in reminiscences: a gas holder behind Bath Place; a gas tap in front of Barnet Corn Exchange; the retort house on Victoria Lane.

Piped water was brought in from outside the district, but before pipes were laid within Chipping Barnet (and in supplement to the many private wells) water was drawn from a well where Ravenscourt Gardens now stand, and transported in a large barrow on wheels. In 1875 some of the

residents of the Hadley Highstone enclave then still within Cockfosters parish approached Enfield Board of Health about arranging water supply from the Barnet Company. They were willing to pay their share of the connection costs but the Company's manager made further 'enquiries from the Inhabitants and finds that they have no desire to have Water laid on to their premises if they are to pay for it'.

Electricity was becoming a serious option by the century's end. The North Metropolitan Power Distribution Company was formed in 1899 and fairly quickly overtook various local authority plans. Barnet Local Board obtained a provisional order in 1893 and, as Barnet UD, another for its now extended area in 1900, but immediately transferred both to Northmet, which opened Barnet generating station at the foot of Tapster Street the same year. East Barnet, which had had a provisional order since 1879, proved more resistant, and in 1903 tried instead to obtain sanction for a £14,000 loan to establish its own scheme. 752 ratepayers, representing over half the rateable value, objected that this would be a far dearer option, and the UD instead struck a favourable deal with Northmet. The company ended at nationalisation in 1948.

139. Victoria Cottage Hospital on its Barnet Hill site. After the hospital moved to Wood Street, the Queen Elizabeth's Girls' School, seen here in the background, expanded over the site.

140. Victoria Hospital in Wood Street, with its classical architecture under Second World War camouflage.

HEALTH CARE

An infirmary wing was added to the workhouse in 1895, and when the workhouse itself was closed in 1939 *(see pp. 64-5)* the infirmary continued as a Public Assistance Hospital. It became part of the new National Health Service from 1948 and changed its name to Barnet General Hospital in 1951. Until the NHS there were no free hospitals outside the workhouse, and the money for the Victoria Hospital was raised by public subscription as a memorial to the royal jubilee. It opened on Barnet Hill in 1888 and moved to Wood Street in 1923. When the NHS was founded it became part of Barnet General, but was retained as the Maternity Hospital until closure in 1988.

LONDONERS

Until the 1780s London was always a net killer, maintaining its population numbers by immigration. Places outside were therefore accurately seen as healthier, and particularly if sited on high well-drained plateaus. Only the very rich could live on the Barnet-Hadley plateau and commute, but others could take occasional advantage. Samuel, the London citizen's child in *Dialogue against the pestilence* (1573, *see p. 29*), was one of many wet-nursed at Barnet.

FOUNDLINGS

Foundlings too were sometimes sent for wet-nursing (although the survival rates were pitiful), but Barnet also briefly hosted a branch of the Foundling Hospital. In 1762 the governors at Coram's Fields in Bloomsbury accepted a proposal by Mrs West of Barnet to rent a house at Barnet for 40 children; in the event it was only fitted up for twelve girls, but so few were sent that when economies were needed it was an obvious victim. In 1768 the 'long coach' returned the children to London and Hadley parish took over the house, furniture and fittings as a replacement workhouse.

THE CHILDREN'S NURSING HOME

The plateau remained a good place for convalescence. A children's home for 'Surgical cases leaving the London hospitals which are not eligible for ordinary convalescent homes but which even more than ordinary cases require fresh air with special skilled treatment in convalescence' started in Granville Road in May 1890 and moved in 1891 to Park Road. Both were the homes of Katherine Pawling, the nurse who was sister-in-charge until her death in 1923, and both were too small. A building fund was started in 1905 and in 1911 a

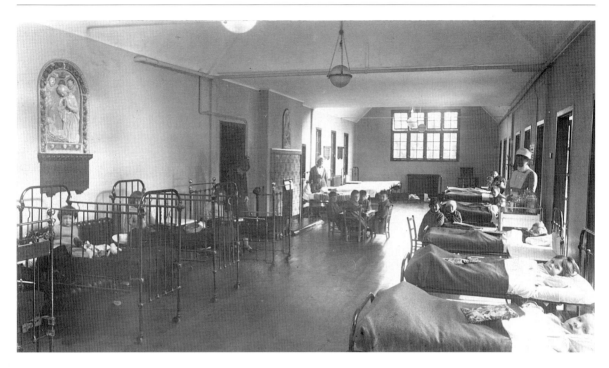

141. A ward in the Children's Hospital at Hadley, probably in the 1920s.

purpose-built hospital was opened at Hadley on land leased (like so many other local benefits) from the Straffords at Wrotham Park. After the Second World War because of general improvements in health and medicine the number of convalescents dwindled, and although there was still a demand for long-term heart- and post-polio-care, when the lease fell in in 1960 it was considered impracticable to renew it. The building became a home for the elderly.

OSSULTON CONVALESCENT HOME
The Mildmay Mission owes its origins to the annual conferences begun by Rev William Pennefather while he was incumbent of Christ Church Barnet (1852-64). Almost coincidentally, the mission established a home at Hadley in 1883 for convalescents from the East and South London Missions and the Mildmay Hospitals. Almost, because the owner at first refused to lease for such a purpose, relenting only when told it was for Pennefather's work: 'Yes, for if ever there was a saint on earth it was Mr.Pennefather'. The home was founded by the Earl and Countess of Tankerton in memory of their eldest son, Lord Ossulton.

142. The south-eastern side of Hadley Green. Ossulton House, one of Hadley's wealth of Georgian houses, is third from the left. Further down is the remarkable Gothic entrance to Hadley Infant School, demolished in 1933.

143. Tudor Hall, the original Queen Elizabeth's School, seen here in a watercolour painted c.1800.

Education, Education....

It is impossible to do justice to all the schools of the area, or to take sufficient count of all the various organisational changes. Before 1870, when primary education became compulsory, provision was patchy and free schools were usually church foundations, although places for the poor were also sometimes endowed in fee-paying establishments. The 1870 Act also allowed the formation of secular School Boards to establish schools in area where the existing provision was inadequate. Not least because the existing provision was largely Church of England, this was an initiative supported by nonconformists and resisted by Anglicans. Chipping Barnet never had a School Board, but East Barnet's (which included New Barnet) was formed in 1893, with East Barnet National School declining to join. From 1902 county councils became the education authorities for their areas, and increasingly active. The extension of free secondary schools undermined the necessity for the plethora of 19th-century private ones. The interwar population increase area saw a corresponding increase in

provision, but never (some things never change) adequately resourced. In the mid-1920s Potters Road School was holding classes in the porch and the girls' cloakroom – the latter since 'the admission of 15 extra children from the Poor Law Institution with no extra staff'. In 1965 the new London Borough of Barnet replaced Herts County Council as the area's education authority.

QUEEN ELIZABETH'S SCHOOL FOR BOYS

A legacy to Thomas Aps 'who teaches the boys' at Barnet is recorded in 1448 but nothing else is known, and if the Holy Trinity guild, like many such, was involved in education, no record remains. The first firm documentation for any school in the area comes in 1573 with a royal charter for establishing 'the Free Grammar School of Queen Elizabeth' at Barnet, although that was the extent of the queen's involvement, the endowment was raised locally and was always inadequate, and 'free' only amounted to free of church control. The detailed regulations of 1634 show cheaper rates for Barnet boys than for outsiders, but even locals had to pay 2s admission fee and £1 per annum 'unless their parents or friends will voluntarily give more'. In 1637 it was agreed to admit four children 'towardly and docile, of poor parents [to] have their learning and education gratis', and the number of free places was extended over time.

The curriculum was daunting but limited: grammar meant Latin (there were punishments for speaking English in the upper forms), with the attendant rhetoric and writing, and religion included thrice-daily prayers and compulsory church attendance at St John's. Even at the end of the 18th century one of the rare nonconformist pupils was 'not a little persecuted by the other boys'. Well before then grammar schools had lost their way, sticking to the old curriculum even though the use of Latin in administration and literature had declined. Indeed a ruling of 1805 held that no endowed grammar school could add new subjects such as mathematics and modern languages. This was not overturned until 1840, but in 1825 the Barnet governors relatively bravely decided 'that the boys should be taught writing, arithmetic, geography and the Latin grammar, and to read the Holy Scriptures'.

They were in fact desperate. Queen Elizabeth's School had neither the endowment nor the site to attract the aristocracy; middle class parents wanted a more useful education, private schools were springing up to supply it, and railways encouraged choice. The level of corporal punishment was also an issue. Flogging was carried out at the whipping post in the hall, and although the rules insisted that there should not be 'immoderate correction', Headmaster Thomas Cox's enthusiasm reached the ears of Dickens, who sent an undercover reporter and then in 1851 wrote the very thinly disguised *A Free (and Easy) School*. Luckily Queen Elizabeth's was not alone: Royal Commissions were at work in the 1860s (visiting Barnet in 1866), and in 1869 the Endowed Schools Act was passed. Under a Scheme of 1873 Queen Elizabeth's, helped with money from the Jesus Charity, embarked on its New Foundation, inviting both day boys and boarders to extended buildings and a curriculum which included bookkeeping, mathematics, French and drawing.

Through governors and scholarships from public elementary schools, the new Scheme and its 1888 revision brought QE into contact with the (new) state educational sector. From 1889 onwards Exchequer funds were increasingly made available via the new county councils for school improvements, and it was thus that Queen Elizabeth's obtained its first science laboratory in 1891.

Particularly from 1918 county councils had considerable powers to assist secondary schools in their area, but with increased control the obvious quid pro quo. QE, with its inadequate premises and endowment, benefited greatly, and it was Herts CC which provided most of the new school, which opened on its current site in 1932.

E.H. Jenkins, Headmaster from 1930-62, was in no doubt that he saw a sea-change, not in 1932 but in the 1950s. From 1930-8 the staff 'struggled, successfully, despite some uncomprehending opposition, to establish good standards'; from 1938-48 the successful struggle was to maintain standards despite war and post-war shortages. But his last period was the first in reverse, an unsuccessful struggle 'against a sort of national decline, wherein public spirit, keenness, good manners, and even good morals not merely fell away, but were even decried in favour of self-interest, material advantages and loose conduct'. Those who were young at the time saw (and still see) things differently, but it is noteworthy that the losses he laments are now normally ascribed to the 1960s or 1980s. As discussed at the start of this book, the point of transition from the past to the present is always problematic.

QUEEN ELIZABETH'S GIRLS' SCHOOL
As the 1869 Act intended, Queen Elizabeth's School's 1873 Scheme made provision for girls, and the Governors were willing enough, but local parents showed so little desire to pay fees for their daughters that it seemed unlikely that a viable school could be started. Finally after mounting pressure, if not from parents then from the local authorities, premises were rented and a Head appointed in summer 1888. At the boys' prize-giving that year it was remarked that a new girls' grammar school allied to an ancient boys' foundation was 'almost an innovation', although at least twenty other girls' public schools had by then been founded.

Forty girls started on Barnet Hill in 1888, but the innovation was still considerable and in 1895 the school was only saved from closure by a staff buy-out. Thereafter it prospered, and in 1898 with 115 pupils for the first time surpassed the boys' numbers. In 1902, in order to share county council grants, it came back into the Queen Elizabeth fold, and in the interwar decades expanded over neighbouring sites.

CHURCH AND CHARITY SCHOOLS

In 1727 Elizabeth Allen bequeathed all her lands to endow a free school in which all the poor children in Barnet, male and female, would learn English (ie reading) as far as the Bible, writing, and arithmetic as far as the rule of three. The money was subverted into QE School's funds (QE made something of a habit of this) until 1823, but was then reclaimed and, with assistance from the National Society, the Elizabeth Allen school opened in Wood Street as a National (that is Anglican) School in 1824. It closed in 1974. Christ Church school opened next to its church's site in 1844, with the Alston Road buildings following in 1880; the whole school moved to Byng Road during the 1960s. To counter Anglican dominance, there was a small British (that is Nonconformist) School in Moxon Street from 1835-1933, and another in Union Street from c.1847-66. (The Union Street school is sometimes dated from the mid-1850s, but must be the British School with 40 pupils adjoining the Independent Chapel listed in Upton's Survey of 1847-8. The confusion has arisen because the Survey describes the Moxon Street school, with 80 pupils, only as 'Infant School, founded by E.Durant Esquire'.) There was also a ragged (or charitably-funded free) school, probably in Union Street, from 1856. Partly because the Ragged School Union was only

opened to schools outside London in 1867 and its records are fragmentary, little is known about the Barnet one, but in 1869 it was a day school with 90 children on the books and an average attendance of 60, taught by one paid teacher and three paid monitors.

In East Barnet the churchwardens were paying a clergyman to teach 'the children of the Inhabitants...letters and good maners' in 1631, and there was a village school, run in a cottage, in 1763. A continuous history only starts, though, from 1822, when the National Society made a grant 'for the fitting up of a daily school for 56 boys and 56 girls'. The school moved to its current premises in 1872, a rebuilding perhaps spurred by the founding in 1871 of a National School linked to St James' in New Barnet.

Hadley was remarkably well supplied with early schools. One for girls was started in 1737 by subscription, and books and spinning wheels purchased; various charitable bequests followed, and it was re-established as a charity school in 1780. In 1800 it became a school of industry (effectively practical education for future servants), and by 1814 had 20 pupils being educated free and another 30 paying 2d a week. Surprisingly, the first school for poor boys was later, a Sunday school started in 1787. A nonconformist started a day school in 1799 but when he died it became

144. A late 19th-century photograph of a class at Highstone School.

145. A picture which exactly matches the name of the Boys' Farm Home. On the extreme right is the elaborate family monument in St Mary's churchyard to Sir Simon Haughton Clarke of Oak Hill (d.1832), so placed as to be visible from Oak Hill's windows.

a National (Anglican) School, and by 1819 had 20 pupils being educated free and about 60 paying 2d a week. The girls' school became associated with the boys' in 1832, when both moved to new buildings on Hadley Common (rebuilt in 1943). There was also a Church of England infants' school on Hadley Green from 1850 to 1922, and another at Highstone (and thus attached to Christ Church, Cockfosters) from 1857 until *c*.1914.

CHURCH FARM INDUSTRIAL SCHOOL
The founders in 1857 of a home for destitute boys in London decided that a country Home was necessary, and Lt. Col. Gillum, a relative, bought a suitable farmhouse next to East Barnet church. The Boys' Farm Home started with four boys in 1860, accelerated to 24 by 1864, and became independent of the London Home in 1868. By 1876 numbers had risen to 79. The boys, some supported through middle-class charity and others sent by the poor law unions and courts, were taught trades such as tailoring as well as farm work, and also had such pleasures as sport, music and scouting. The institution became an approved school in 1933 (when the licensed number rose to 105), but it moved away to Godstone in 1937 (and closed in 1980). Col. Gillum, an early patron

of William Morris's circle, commissioned Philip Webb and Webb's friend C.G.Vinall to build extensions to the farm buildings, and Webb to build him a house, Trevor Park. This has gone although the gatehouse (lamentably altered) still stands.

PRIVATE SCHOOLS
Private schools have always come and gone, often barely (if at all) outlasting their founders. Hadley, and particularly its girls, was again surprisingly well supplied. An academy for gentlemen's sons was started at Ludgrove in the mid-17th century, but closed around 1680; a boys' school founded by David Garrow flourished in the mid-18th century; by 1819 there was a day school for 60 girls, of whom 43 came from outside Hadley; and in 1833 there was a girls' day and boarding school run by Baptists.

In the second half of the 19th century suburban growth, particularly in New Barnet, brought many more fee-paying schools. Around 1880 boys' possibilities included Lyonsdown Middle-Class School, 'Pupils prepared for the Navy and Public Schools, Preliminary Law, the Civil Service, Oxford and Cambridge Local Examinations'; Cowley College, which moved to New Barnet in 1876 and whose Principal was 'Assisted by a

146. Silesia College c.1880.

Competent Staff of highly qualified English and Foreign Tutors'; and Silesia College. This started as Silesia House Patriotic Orphan Home for Boys, specifically for orphans of soldiers killed in the Crimean War (1854-6); by 1871 it was known as Silesia School, and after it was acquired by Mr Russell around 1879 became Silesia College. It closed during the first decade of the 20th century and the house it had occupied, Oakmede on Bells Hill, was a victim of a landmine in1940.

There was also a range of schools for girls, including Verulam Lodge Establishment for Young Ladies in Station Road, and Raincliffe Ladies' College in Lyonsdown. These were unconcerned with preparation for careers but, in the words of a Raincliffe College advertisement, 'particular attention is paid to the Accomplishments. Inclusive Terms, arranged to embrace English, French, German, Music, Singing and Drawing'. The Sisters of St Martha founded a fee-paying girls' convent school at the western end of Wood Street *c.*1904. As the school enlarged, it moved to Park Road, New Barnet, then returned to Wood Street in 1914, taking over the premises of the by then defunct Community of St Andrew. A senior school was established at Mount House in Hadley in 1947 and the community moved to Hadley Bourne in 1949. The school still flourishes but the community has shrunk, and is today (2002) looking for smaller premises.

BARNET COLLEGE

Access to university education was very limited until the passing of the 1944 Education Act. By the later 19th-century efforts were being made to extend some of its benefits, and the London Society for the Extension of University Teaching, which started in 1876, initiated a Barnet Centre in 1889. This provided a range of lectures, but at fee-levels which ensured a purely middle-class attendance. In 1892 it merged with the Barnet Technical Instruction Committee to become the Barnet University Extension and Technical Instruction Society, which continued the general lectures but also, with grants from Hertfordshire CC, began to offer some serious technical classes. The 1902 Education Act placed all Technical and Further Education under Herts CC as the new Local Education Authority. Classes continued to be held in various places, but especially Byng Road School, until Queen Elizabeth Boys moved to its new premises in 1932, and Herts CC bought the old buildings – since then much altered and enlarged. The college was renamed Barnet College in 1963 and transferred to the new London Borough of Barnet in 1965.

147. *Raincliffe Ladies' College, in an undated photograph.*

148. *The Barnet Art Class exhibition of 1906, part of the expanding field of further education.*

Social life

SOCIETIES

Barnet and Hadley have been, and still are, full of clubs and societies – far too many to cover even summarily. Those chosen here are hopefully both representative and interesting, but they are also fairly well documented. Societies of all sorts have a bad habit of throwing out their archive and then, particularly if an anniversary approaches, wishing that they hadn't. Local newspapers are an excellent additional source but are unindexed, and even the earliest, the *Barnet Press*, was not founded until 1859.

HORTICULTURE

Minute books can be unexpectedly riveting, and one of the best is the solitary volume of the Barnet Horticultural and Floricultural Society, running from 1837-43. After a couple of exploratory meetings held at the White Hart in Barnet, the society was established in 1837, apparently with the sole aim of holding shows. The rules included the following:

'1st The affairs of this Society shall be conducted by a President, [in this case Captain Trotter of Dyrham Park], Vice-Presidents [Rev Mr Elwin, Baron Dimsdale and Enoch Durant esq], Treasurer, Committee of 20, namely 10 Practical Men and 10 Amateurs, and a Secretary;
4th That Members shall pay not less than 7s 6d per annum;
8th That there be two or more public Shows every year;
12th That the Exhibitors be divided into 3 Classes. 1st Amateurs, not cultivating Flowers for sale or profit; 2nd Gentlemen's Gardeners entering Flowers in their own names; 3rd Nurserymen, large Growers, and all persons growing Plants for sale etc.'

An addendum is equally revealing: 'Subscribers may invite Cottagers to send the productions of their Gardens, and Prizes will be awarded to the best of Specimens. Their name and place of abode, certified and signed by a Subscriber, will entitle them to exhibit'.

The first two shows were planned for 27 June and 19 September 1838, although the June one had to be altered 'on account of the coronation'. Amateurs in June could exhibit various flowers, including geraniums in six varieties. The gentlemen's gardeners also had a range of hothouse classes, including orchids, pineapples, melons,

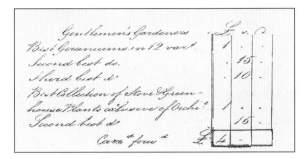

149. The start of the list of categories and prizes for gentlemen's gardeners at the Barnet Horticultural and Floricultural Society's first show in June 1838.

grapes, peaches and nectarines. The nurserymen were restricted to the best collection of named roses, and the 'best rare or new plant that may be considered worthy'. Cottagers could submit a collection of flowers, but were expected to concentrate on cabbages, lettuces, onions, peas, kidney beans and potatoes, with added prizes from the president and secretary of a store pig and a set of garden tools for the best two collections of vegetables. The show may have been all too successful, for in August 'The Committee strongly recommend those Gents named to manage the [September] Show, to take efficient measures to prevent any intrusion into the Hall etc previous to the hour named for the admission of the Public'.

Nothing could better encapsulate the horticulture of the period, the professional gentlemen and nurserymen experimenting with species and producing fruit which a century and more later was still a rarity, and the treatment of the cottagers. A few ladies became members, as did some non-local nurserymen. The final entry in May 1843 records the admission of Mr Marshal, gardener to the Rev Henry Reid; and the later volumes are sadly missing.

SOCIALISING

Some societies had little purpose beyond good fellowship, even though their names, Amicable, Constitutional and so forth, might suggest something more. The Barnet Amicable Society, founded in 1836, sounds like a mutual aid association (*see p. 68*) but its only activities were a weekly meeting at the Red Lion, an annual dinner, and, ultimately, outings. The income to fund the dinners (which cost £1 a head in 1836) came from fines for non-attendance and other offences. The fine for betting during club hours was doubled in

150. Gardens have always also provided a frame for general socialising. This surely distinctive but still unidentified scene was taken by S. Hockett & Co., photographers in New Barnet.

151. The bill for the Barnet Amicable Society's annual dinner in 1912.

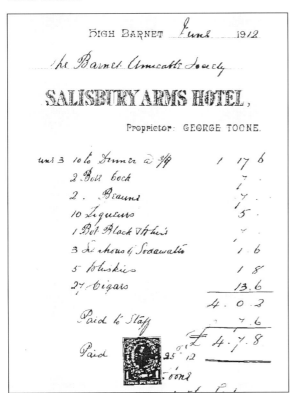

1873 from 6d to 1s, but the previous fine of 1d a game on 'Members playing at Cards, Chess, Draughts, or any other Game during Club-hours', more a fee than a penalty, vanished. Serious fines of 5s (25p) were imposed for divulging the affairs of the society, and for using obscene language, clarified in 1873 as 'swearing or using any pro-fane obscene or indecent language or conducting himself in an offensive manner towards any member of the Society during Club hours'. The Barnet Amicable was a typical club set up by local traders who wanted to meet socially but not in a public bar. Although at first glance similar to Rotary, these groups never developed either the representative or the charitable dimension.

SKILLS AND SELF-IMPROVEMENT

Apart from church groups – a major category – and limited social clubs such as the Barnet Amicable, most groups, clubs and societies were founded to foster interests and self-improvement as well as socialising. Their number and range increased dramatically from the second half of the 19th century, as knowledge and technology and the thirst for them grew, and the population, especially in New Barnet, expanded. The thirst for self-improvement was not restricted to any particular group, but class barriers remained firmly in place, with working men's clubs on the one hand and societies with high fees on the other. The Hadley Memorial Hall, also known as the Iron Hut, was built for Victoria's jubilee in 1887 as a working men's club, and is listed in 1920s directories as Highstone Reading Room and Working Men's Club. It was acquired by the Girls' Club in 1932, and moved on to become a general village hall in 1948. It reopened after rebuilding in 1988. An original iron hut can still be seen, though, at Arkley, with 'Arkley Working Men's Club, 1902' inscribed above the door.

THE LIT

On a different tack, the New Barnet Young Men's Mutual Improvement Society opened under combined nonconformist auspices in 1874. Despite lightening the name – Young Men's Society, or Young Men's Association – it was not a runaway success and nearly foundered. In 1880, though, it was agreed that ladies too could be admitted, 29 were promptly elected, the problem was solved, and the group evolved into the New Barnet Literary and Debating Society – the Lit. Even so, until 1888 lady members were not allowed to speak at the meetings (if they felt they absolutely had to contribute, they did so in writing and their words were read out by a man), and following a near-fatal split over the disestablishment of the

Churches of England and Scotland, discussion of religious and political matters was banned from 1882 until 1966. Despite its longevity and success, the society follows the usual pattern: peak membership of over 370 in 1907, gradual slippage from the 1920s, just below 200 in 1924 and 170 in 1930, 100 by 1950, and 50 at its centenary.

THE BARNET DISTRICT INDUSTRIAL EXHIBITIONS

The New Barnet nonconformist churches also took the lead in sponsoring the Barnet District Industrial Exhibition – victim of a shift in word-meaning since the industry was entirely domestic, featuring needlework, painting and so on. The exhibition also included competitions between the nonconformist choirs of both New and Chipping Barnet. It was an annual event, held every April from 1888 until certainly 1910 and probably 1914, and the sheer amount of industry involved was, as always, notable. The show ran each year for four days, with over sixty classes and, from 1893, an accompanying newspaper, the *Barnet District Industrial Star*. These activities shade into technical classes and the activities of the forerunners of Barnet College (*see p. 114*).

152. *Part of the prize list for the 1904 Barnet District Industrial Exhibition, which contained 61 classes.*

NATURAL HISTORY

The Barnet Natural History Society started in 1905, hoping 'to promote and popularise a taste for the study of natural history and archaeology, to develop and foster social and friendly intercourse among naturalists, archaeologists and others of congenial tastes, and generally to encourage a love of the beautiful in nature'. It would hold monthly evening meetings each winter 'when informal papers on scientific matters and natural phenomena of local interest will be read by the members, objects (eggs, moths etc) collected during the season exhibited and discussed, photographic slides and natural objects shown, meteorological reports handed in etc'. Natural history societies were among the few which sometimes crossed class barriers, but this one charged 2s 6d a meeting, roughly a quarter of an unskilled man's weekly wage. Nevertheless the society got off to a rip-roaring start, with around 150 members within the year (and some of them women). It continued successfully too until 1939, but at the outbreak of war all public meetings were banned and many halls requisitioned, and this society was one of those which never reassembled. To found anything similar today would be unimaginable: it is a classic example of the profit and loss account of the parochial versus the global village.

LOCAL HISTORY

Local history is one of the few interests which remains necessarily local, and it has therefore survived rather better. B.R. Leftwich's letter to the *Barnet Press* in 1927 was prompted by his concern that 'Barnet is fast becoming a suburb of London; all its old landmarks are fast disappearing, and there is a danger that in a few years' time all trace of them may be lost'. He suggested founding a society 'to collect all documents relating to the Barnets', by (pre-photocopier) transcription and photography as well as by actual

153. *'Lord' George Sanger's circus had its winter quarters at Finchley until Sanger's murder there in 1911, so that processions such as this were a regular local spectacle.*

collection, and the Barnet Record Society was duly formed. Despite inflation since 1905, the entry fee this time was a non-prohibitive 2s 6d a year for working members. There were monthly meetings, to which members should bring something of local interest, and excursions. Membership climbed steadily, from 60 in the first year to 180 in 1936 and 226 in 1957, and although it fell in the 1960s, stands today (2002) at around 300. The society, renamed the Barnet and District Local History Society in 1967, has the most obvious presence of any because of its museum; the collection started in 1928, and has been charmingly (if not exactly spaciously) housed in 31 Wood Street since 1938.

DRAMA

There is also still life in local drama and music, but once again wider horizons have fundamentally shifted the balance. Not that the past was ever static. The 'Great Room' upstairs in the Red Lion where Pepys ate his cheesecakes in 1667 *(see ill. 36)*, later became the Assembly Rooms, used both for public meetings and as a theatre. According to a report in the *Barnet Gazette* in 1858, 'The Barnet Theatre was largely patronised in particular by the late much-respected family of Wrotham Park and the then residents at Trent Park, by whom plays were frequently selected "By Special Desire".' The less exalted could also enjoy the theatre 'very neatly fitted up after the London style', and the annual appearances of Osborne's Company over many years. But 'the fittings were taken down and sold nearly fifty years ago, from which period the drama rapidly declined in Barnet, and has now become obsolete. The last performance in this room took place on 30 March, 1835, the pieces being The Rivals, 5th Act of Richard III, and Timour the Tartar, by a company of strollers of considerable ability, but whose exertions over a season of several weeks were nightly productive only of a beggarly account of empty benches'.

Like the professional touring companies, local amateur productions have had a variously successful history. During his 33 years as a reviewer, from 1945-78, Bill Gelder saw 78 groups over a somewhat wider area, most of which had disbanded by the 1980s. But as he noted, even before modern pressures the Barnet Amateur Dramatic Society ceased to exist in 1881 'for want of sufficient support'. At the other end of the scale, the Barnet Arts Club (since 1965 the Barnet Borough Arts Club), founded in 1921 and the oldest in his

book, still flourishes. So too does the Old Bull Theatre, founded in 1975.

Two of the disbanded groups were offshoots – the Dramatic Section of the New Barnet Lit, which started in 1920 and closed in 1957, and the St Peter's Players, a church group. Beyond the regular groups there were also many special drama and music events, ranging from the choir competitions and musical performances at the Barnet District Industrial Exhibition through to concerts of various sorts. The concerts could be ends in themselves, but were often part of the endless fundraising activities which, apart from their intrinsic worth, helped mop up quantities of middle-class female energy. Many such activities were church-based, but others were more generally philanthropic, such as the Evening of Songs and Fairy Tales held in aid of the Barnet Provident Club in 1911. Miss Dora Byfield, one of the organisers, was the capable daughter of East Barnet Council's Clerk who, had she been a man, would have had an equally successful career. As it was, a whole range of local organisations (and some appeals for wider charities) benefited from her voluntary involvement.

154. The programme for the charity performance in 1911. The evening included Sleeping Beauty, and songs and stories from six improvident pierrots.

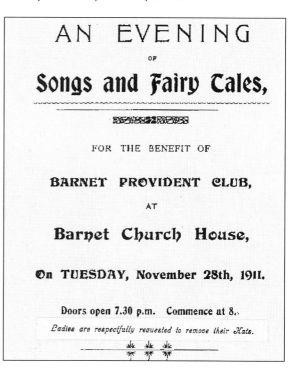

155. *Perhaps a similar entertainment but the other side of the Great War: a British Legion concert party in 1925.*

MUSIC

As well as the church choirs and the various concerts, there were many other music groups, including the Barnet Amateur Orchestral Society which played at the Barnet District Industrial Exhibition in 1909, and the Arkley Music Society, also flourishing in 1909. Best known is the Barnet Band, formed in 1889 as the High Barnet Foresters' Brass Band and known for years as the Barnet Town Band *(ill. 156)*. It played originally at the Green Man, but in 1905 began to play on Hadley Green and in Barnet High Street, and in 1911 acquired silver instruments. It also acquired a march, 'On Hadley Green', written by an amateur composer, Mr Reginald Green, and dedicated to the band. Woodwinds were added in the mid-1980s.

SPORT

There is still plenty of local involvement in sport, but much has changed. Part of the change is in the sports themselves. The horse racing, cock fights and gambling at Barnet Fair have ended, as has bare-knuckle fighting. Fox hunts too have gone, although beagles for hunting on foot were kept at Hadley in the 19th century, the Enfield Chase Hunt used to meet at Old Fold Farm *(see also illustration 168)*, and Major Smith-Bosanquet's hunt at Arkley featured in the *Illustrated Sporting and Dramatic News* in 1921.

BARE-KNUCKLE FIGHTING

Thanks to convenient access from London, the various advantages of the inns, fair and raceground, and the large number of butchers (the most pugilistic trade) with their London links, Barnet and Hadley figure very prominently in the history of bare-knuckle fighting. In 1747 a London debut was publicised thus: 'I, Joseph Line from Hadley...where I am the terror of all around'; and in 1761 Nicholas Grady, 'the little Barnet poulterer' fought on Barnet Common, as did one of the Clare Market butchers a decade later. At some local bouts stakes and cords sufficed or the spectators formed the ring, but the racecourse (with its grandstand) was also sometimes used. In 1787 the celebrated Daniel Mendoza fought there at the instigation of the Prince of Wales (the future George IV), who was in the audience along with his brother, the Duke of York, and 5,000 others. Mendoza won, and his opponent was taken to the Red Lion to have his wounds dressed. Several of the local inns, including the Mitre, were also used for training.

Despite such endorsement, most bare-knuckle fighting was illegal, and could also generate major unrest. The Easter 1787 Quarter Sessions ordered that a decree appear in the London newspapers and 'a sufficient number of copies thereof [be] printed and stuck in all public places near to the

156. *The Barnet Town Prize Band, on a postcard sent in 1906 (see p.121).*

said town of Barnet'. It said:

> 'Information having been given to this Court, that large numbers of people have lately, and at different times, assembled together at or near the town of Chipping Barnet...for the purpose of fighting pitched battles, and that more such meetings are intended...this Court, considering that all such unlawful assemblies occasion great riots, tumults and disorders, wherever they are held, and that they tend much to disturb the public peace, doth recommend to His Majesty's Justices of the Peace for this county to attend wherever such meetings may be...for the purpose of preventing the like evil'.

This presumably ties in with the bill paid at the Midsummer Sessions for the expenses of the magistrates who had met at the Mitre to suppress an intended riot: the total for forty dinners, beer, wine, punch, horses, tobacco, and servants amounted to £6 9s 6d. Such inducements apart, enforcement was seldom easy or enjoyable. Usually if a JP appeared planned fights simply moved elsewhere, but in 1792 would-be spectators on Barnet Common 'obstinately, unlawfully and riotously' (and violently) refused to disperse.

Bare-knuckle fighting went into terminal decline during the 19th century, and improved policing coupled with the advent of railways sent many contests further afield. But the 1880s saw a splendid local swan-song. In 1881 a ten-foot ring was formed and a fight started in a secluded 'delightful spot' in Hadley Wood, but the police arrived and the crowd moved off to Potters Bar; here the police again arrived, and the crowd boarded a train for Oakleigh Park; the train failed to stop, so the crowd alighted at Wood Green and headed into Alexandra Park. The return bout in 1882 was fought, symptomatically, with gloves under the Marquis of Queensberry's rules. In 1883 the crowd came by train to New Barnet and walked up into Hadley Woods, where the spectators stood shoulder to shoulder to form the ring and the fight began. This time, though, the Inspector of Barnet Police had been forewarned, his men were hidden in the woods, and as time for the second round was called they sprang out and managed to capture both the fighters and several spectators. In court the defendants cheerfully denied being involved in a prize-fight, insisting variously that they were just settling differences with their hands, watching to see fair play, or simply walking in the woods. They were disbelieved, but let off lightly.

157. *A dancing bear in Barnet High Street in the 1920s. As with boxing, worry about barbarity is a recent phenomenon.*

158. The foot race of 1845 reported in the Illustrated London News.

FOOT RACING

Some runs were entirely solitary: there were three similar wagers in 1808, 1812 and 1814 that the contestant could get the 22 miles from London to Barnet and back inside two and a half hours – and they each managed it with, respectively, eight minutes, half a minute, and 28 minutes to spare. A slightly different event took place in 1845 from the Duke of York at Gannick Corner, just north of Hadley, when a mile was measured out southwards along the Great North Road, and two competitors, Sheppard and Jackson (alias the American Deer), ran up and down it for an hour. Both covered the first mile in about six minutes, Sheppard collapsed at the turn of the tenth, but Jackson went on to cover 'eleven miles all but 100 yards, over a heavy road'.

CYCLING

After the initial wobbles of the penny-farthings, from the 1880s 'safety' bikes opened up whole new possibilities of affordable recreation. They chimed with a new concern about what would now be termed a healthy lifestyle, proving par-ticularly useful to women in the battle against breath-restricting corsets, and to both sexes in allowing unchaperoned group outings. Sunday spins, which did not cause anyone else to labour, also helped weaken the restrictions of sabbatarianism, at least among the more liberal sects, allowing people to enjoy their one day of leisure. No wonder that so many of the memoirs and photographs of the period feature bicycles.

Cycling was hard work – no gears, no pneu-matic tyres until 1890, and no smooth road sur-faces until after the advent of motoring. Never-theless the 1880s had their lycra-clad equivalents in the North Road Cycling Club, founded in 1885 to encourage and facilitate long-distance riding. The initial programme included a medal for rid-ing 250 miles in 24 hours but most of the races were local – in 1886 a series of ten-mile handicaps from Hadley Highstone to Ridge and back yielded a fastest time of 36 minutes 27 seconds. Both bicyclists and tricyclists were eligible, and mem-bership grew from 37 in the first year to 102 by 1889 and 178 by 1905. Only once was a woman allowed to compete, who covered 25 miles on her tricycle in 1888 before retiring.

159. *Members of the North Road Cycling Club in the 1890s outside their regular meeting place, the Two Brewers at Hadley. Two of Hadley Brewery's chimneys are visible on the left.*

The club's other activities were firmly male-oriented. The opening run of the 1887 season was a cycle paper-chase in March from the Tally Ho! in Finchley to the Two Brewers at Hadley, where tea was followed by boxing and a smoking concert. Cycling programmes were impossible in winter, and boxing was the winter substitute, so much so that members also formed the North Road Boxing Club. Meeting every Saturday at the Two Brewers, after tea the evening was spent in a great variety of games, but especially boxing (including professional instruction) and tug-of-war. In later years the winter quarters moved to the Old Salisbury, which was also from 1904 the starting point of the London-York run (begun in 1891 from St Martin-le-Grand in London).

MOTORING
Cars are the least healthy form of outdoor recreation imaginable, but did of course extend all sorts of freedoms, for the lucky few in the pioneering phase from around 1900, and for the masses, at least potentially, once Henry Ford had revolutionised production. (The first Model T Fords were manufactured in Detroit in 1909 and in Manchester in 1911.) It was more fun before ownership became so universal that the roads became clogged, the situation since the 1980s.

SWIMMING
When the Gas and Water Company's tank on Victoria Lane became redundant it was used for a while as a scratch swimming pool. The YMCA branch, opened at 121 High Street Barnet in 1902, added a pool in 1908, according to the *YMCA News* 'an immense attraction, both to members and to outside clubs', but neither the branch nor the pool seems to have survived the First World War. Less certainly, it was believed at Swain's that Bath Place took its name from former public baths which were incorporated into the letterpress printing department.

CRICKET
Occasional matches were being played by the mid-18th century. On 19 July 1749 Herts played Middlesex 'at the Gate Inn Barnet Common' (right on the county boundary), for fifty guineas a side and with bye balls and overthrows allowed. Two years later Barnet and Hadley 'bachelors' issued a challenge to any two parishes within seven miles of Barnet, for not more than 2s 6d a man 'and for the encouragement of the winners, Thomas Sanders of the King's Head at Barnet will give gratis thirteen pairs of silver sleeve buttons'.

Regular local clubs must have been somewhat

160. *Mr Francis and staff outside his premises at the Hadley end of Barnet High Street. FN was a leading Belgian firm, and first produced this particular two-seater in 1914, the probable year of the photograph.*

161. *Hadley Cricket Club, probably in the 1940s.*

later. Monken Hadley Cricket Club was certainly playing on Hadley Common by 1871, when avoiding grazing cattle could still be a problem. Barnet Cricket Club had a ground next to the Great North Road until around 1930, when this became the site of Raydean Road and its neighbours, and the club shifted to the Underhill Playing Fields. A motor mower simultaneously replaced the one drawn by Sydney Etheridge's horse. Etheridge was not only the groundsman but also a former Middlesex and Barnet player, and until 1918 a leading light (like his father and brother) in the Cockfosters Cricket Club.

The Cockfosters club started in August 1873, and played initially both on ground near Christ Church lent by J.D. Burnaby esq and in Trent Park. The latter lies within Enfield, as does Christ Church, but so close to the Barnet and Hadley boundaries that Mr Burnaby's field might have lain in either. On later occasions teams played at Belmont and in Oakhill Park, and although the permanent grounds were and are on the Enfield side, the 1929 lease (which also covered the Cockfosters Bowling Club and the Cockfosters Tennis Club) was made by Cosmo Bevan of West Farm Place. Southgate Borough Council agreed to buy the land, and thus preserved it from development, in 1947, and in January 1948 the club celebrated '75 years of keen, sparkling cricket, backed by good fellowship on the social side' with a dinner-dance at the Salisbury Hotel in Barnet.

GOLF

The unbuilt-up edges of suburbia are ideal for golf courses, and Barnet and Hadley have two. A meeting of the Arkley Music Society heard in March 1909 that a field next to Rowley Green suitable for a nine-hole course could be rented from its owner, Lord Strafford (of Wrotham Park).

162. Football at Market Place in Chipping Barnet c.1788. The hill, which must have complicated the game, is missing from the distinctly foreshortened picture (see p.128).

While the initial levelling was being done part of Arkley Common also became available, and the whole site was officially opened in August. Another 11 acres was leased from the earl in 1923, and in 1929 Barnet Urban District both acquired the earl's land and offered a lease with a further 46 acres provided the Arkley Common land was returned. The club's fees assured exclusivity, but a separate group, known as the Arkley Villagers' Golf Club and in fact part of the Working Men's Club, had restricted rights from the end of the First World War. Around 1930 this group became affiliated to the Artisans' Golf Union, was renamed the Arkley Artisans, and achieved formal recognition.

Although a photograph exists titled 'Golf players on Sunset Fields, Old Fold Manor' and dated 1897, Old Fold Manor Golf Club was not founded until 1910 – within a year of the Arkley Club and also on land leased from Lord Strafford. The club house stands next to the manor house, and is a combination of a c.1820 building with a cleverly matching addition of 1928-9.

FOOTBALL

One of the earliest engravings of football shows eight men playing in Barnet Market Place c.1750 *(ill. 161)*. The earliest clubs, though, date from the mid-19th century, and the rules of Association Football from 1863. By the late 19th century Barnet and Hadley had a plethora of clubs, whose history still needs some disentangling. According to John Adkins, Barnet FC's current historian, the first fixture list to feature 'Barnet Football Club' occurs in 1888, but this had previously been New Barnet, or Woodville, FC, founded in the mid-1880s and playing at Mrs Cook's farm. The club collapsed in 1901, but in 1904 another of the many, Barnet Avenue, dropped the Avenue from its title and became in its turn Barnet FC. Two years later, in 1906, the Alston Works Team renamed itself Barnet Alston, in 1911 it joined forces with Barnet (Avenue) to become Barnet and Alston FC, and in 1918 the name was shortened back to Barnet FC. The club has played at Underhill since 1907 and turned professional in 1965.

Barnet's recent history has been particularly dramatic. It was promoted to the Football League in 1991 and into the 2nd division in 1993, but

163. *Barnet Football Club in 1910, accompanied by the bowler-hatted headmaster of Christ Church School.*

Chairman Stan Flashman's unusual business methods then led to the departure of the long-suffering manager, Barry Fry, and most of the squad. The team was relegated down the divisions from 1994, and out of the league in 2001. The Underhill site, with its famously non-level playing field, is also too small for the necessary stadium improvements, but every suggested alternative is controversial.

CINEMA
Even for the Victorian and Edwardian period the image of every family diligently making its own amusements round the piano is greatly exaggerated. But it is certainly true that for all classes in a world without cinema, radio or television and, for most, little travel, entertainment was far more family- and community-based than now. The first widening of horizons, and corresponding weakening of participatory activity, came with the cinema, from the 1910s until the advent of mass television in the 1950s by far the most popular form of entertainment. Films were something for which people were prepared to travel, so that Finchley as well as Barnet houses feature in local reminiscences. Barnet's own earliest was the Cinema Palace, opened in the silent era in 1912 and renamed the Barnet Cinema in 1926, when it was operating two evening houses and a Saturday matinee. Taken over by the Odeon circuit in 1936 and renamed the Gaumont in 1955, it closed in 1959 to be demolished and replaced by a Waitrose supermarket. Similarly, the Dominion in East Barnet Road, which opened in 1938 with a guest appearance by Gracie Fields, became the Essoldo in 1950 and closed in 1967, also to be replaced by a supermarket.

In New Barnet the Lytton Road Assembly Rooms (built by E. Fergusson Taylor c.1870) were converted into a small cinema, the Hippodrome, which ran for three months in 1925, was relaunched later the same year as the Kinema, and was then replaced with a purpose-built house, the New Barnet Picture Theatre, in 1926. It became the Regal in 1933 and was converted to bingo in 1966 and quasar thereafter, before demolition in 1999. The only local cinema today is the Odeon at Underhill, which opened in purpose-built splendour in 1935 and was converted to a triple-screen complex in 1974.

164. *Since this view was taken before 1926, the cinema in the foreground was still known as the Cinema Palace. Two shops away is the Salisbury Arms before its Brewers' Tudor makeover.*

165. *Barnet Odeon around the time of its opening in 1935.*

166. *A programme for the Abbey Folk Park and Museum, c.1934.*

ABBEY FOLK PARK

In 1934 John Ward established an open-air museum at Hadley Hall, 89 Park Road, New Barnet which featured a prehistoric village, a 13th-century tithe barn from Kent, and a 17th-century well. This became the nucleus of the English Folk Park, to which in 1935 he added an Ethnographical Folk Park. The Princesses Elizabeth and Margaret were among its many delighted visitors. Ward began as an Anglican clergyman, but then transferred to the Orthodox Catholic Church of England, in which within two days in October 1935 he graduated through all the stages from baptism up to priest and bishop. Alongside the museum he also ran a community, the abbey of Christ the King, which shared many of the characteristics of other such sects revolving around charismatic leaders. In May 1945 he was charged with enticement and in October, by now Archbishop of the British Empire of the Orthodox Catholic Church, came close to bankruptcy. He went abroad shortly afterwards. The site continued as an arts centre in various guises. Much of the ethnographic collection was in Cyprus from 1945 and has since 1986 formed part of the Abbey Museum in Queensland, Australia.

Wartimes

Barnet and Hadley appear in the general history books as the site of the Battle of Barnet in 1471 and of General Monk's eventful night in 1660, and also for the location of the Radio Security Service at Arkley from 1940-5. Such a list, of course, underplays the reality of local involvement in wars down the centuries.

THE BATTLE OF BARNET

The Battle of Barnet was actually fought mainly in Hadley, on the open green then known as Gladmore Heath, but battlefields are large places and this one extended back towards St John's at Chipping Barnet as well as eastwards across today's Hadley Common and down the slope to New Barnet. As with so much else in this area's history, it was primarily the main road that dictated the battle site, and it is no coincidence that in the same long drawn-out civil war, known (with a name more romantic than the grim reality) as the Wars of the Roses, two battles had already been fought a little further up the road at St Albans. Richard Neville, Earl of Warwick, whose habit of changing sides had helped earn him the soubriquet of Warwick the Kingmaker, was hurrying south to London at the head of the Lancastrian forces, and stopped overnight 'under an hedgesyde…in array'. Local tradition identifies the hedge with one which still survives on Old Fold golf course, and an exercise in hedgerow dating carried out in the 1970s concluded that this hedge was indeed well established by the 1470s.

The Yorkists under Edward IV also arrived that evening, and at daybreak, despite the fact that it was Easter Sunday and extremely foggy, battle was joined. The fog brought confusion, and a Yorkist victory. A section of Edward's troops was initially routed and fled back to Barnet town, but when the pursuing Lancastrian section returned to the field and to what should have been the Yorkist flank, the battle had swung through an arc. Compounding the mistake, they misread the Lancastrian Earl of Oxford's badge, a star with streams, for Edward's sun with rays, and attacked. The earl and his men, understandably, 'cried Treasonn and fledde away', and although the battle was far from over, Edward's victory was essentially assured. He and his men toasted their victory in Barnet's inns.

The battle was an important turning point, not least because Warwick the Kingmaker was among

167. A charming picture of someone inspecting the Battle of Barnet obelisk on the battlefield at Hadley. It was painted c.1800, before the monument was moved a few yards further north.

168. Warwick's Oak in Hadley village, shown with a hunt on a postcard sent in 1917. The railings were sent for salvage in 1941 and the much decayed tree went soon afterwards.

the dead. Slain 'somewhat fleing', exactly where this happened is unclear. The obelisk at the Highstone which claims to commemorate the spot was not erected until *c.*1740, or roughly 270 years after the event, and was also moved slightly further north *c.*1840. The same commemorative claim was made for Warwick's Oak, this time in the middle of Hadley village, but probably simply because it was obviously old. The bodies of Warwick and other noblemen who died were carried to London, but the common soldiers – a considerable number since Edward had rescinded his usual order to spare them – were buried at the field, and a mortuary chapel erected. Surprisingly, and despite the field known as Dead Men's Bottom and various excavations, no trace of either has ever been found. In 1580 Stow reported having seen the chapel, by then a dwelling house, and there is a rich choice of legends about the site, the strongest of which feature Hermitage Cottage, now within Wrotham Park, and The Mount House, The Priory, and Pymlico House at Hadley.

HADLEY BEACON

The cresset which still adorns the tower of St Mary's at Hadley is still lit on major ceremonial occasions, most recently for the Queen's Golden Jubilee celebrations in June 2002. It is surrounded by a miasma of local legend-making. Prosaically, the caption to a drawing at the Guildhall Library, which was made in 1791 and states that the cresset was put up to commemorate George III's first recovery from madness in 1765, is probably accurate. It was drawn and written within a generation of the alleged occasion, and chimes with what seems to be the first concrete reference, that the cresset was blown down in the great gale of 1 January 1779. It is possible that there had been an earlier beacon at Beacon Hill, whose name may have been in existence by the 1580s, and thus at a time when beacons were part of a national invasion warning system, but various local myths about its use - before the Battle of Barnet; to warn St Albans of attacks up the Lea; to guide travellers through the (surely sky-shrouding) wood of Enfield Chase – are, to put it politely, implausible.

169. Hadley church's cresset, photographed in 1916.

170. General Monk.

GENERAL MONK'S VISIT

As with the battle of 1471, so General Monk's eventful night in Barnet in 1660 was entirely due to the road. On 2 February, in the final phase before the restoration of Charles II, Monk marched southwards from St Albans and stayed overnight at Barnet, probably at the Mitre. One of his chaplains, John Price, recorded that the general 'took up quarters only for himself and his domestique retinue…much business was here dispacht; orders were distributed for our next day's march into town [ie London], and that our soldiers should demean themselves civily in their quarters, and pay for them; for our money held out still'. The alternative scenario if military money had run out hovers like a chill in the air, not least because Price reported that 'The next day, before we came to Highgate, the general drew up his forces, which consisted of four regiments of foot and three of horse their number being 5,800, allowing 1,000 to each regiment of foot and 600 to each regiment of horse, besides officers'.

This time, though, the excitement was limited to Thomas Scot, one of the commissioners sent by Parliament to keep Monk under surveillance, who at around midnight burst in after what must have been a brisk run through the streets, clad only in night gown, cap and slippers, to relay news from London that soldiers there 'were fallen into a high mutiny, and that there was a danger that they would joyn with the [ap]prentices, who cryed upon the streets for a Free Parliament, [and] passionately desired, or rather by his authority required the general immediately to beat his drums and march'. Keeping his head, Monk 'calmly answered him, I will answer for this night's disturbance and be early enough in the morning to prevent any mischief'. He did agree to send a messenger immediately, who reported that the uproar had been soon quashed, thus strengthening the suspicion that Scot's dramatic performance and 'motion for such a hasty march was …an artifice…so as to mingle the soldiers of both armies that they might be the less at the general's devotion'. How all Monk's troops were billeted is hard to imagine, but a century later the War Office billeting returns of 1756 offer a handy guide to the Barnet and Hadley inns (see p. 33).

171. The Barnet Militia with a gun carriage, c.1900.

HOME DEFENCE: THE MILITIA AND VOLUNTEER FORCES

There have been arrangements for home defence since Anglo-Saxon times, but recent systems are usually dated back to the reorganisation of the county militias from 1757. Also known as the Yeomanry, these regiments were raised as required, with a compulsory levy of men placed on each parish. During the Napoleonic Wars, when invasion seemed imminent, provision was also made for raising local volunteer forces, and the two systems continued thereafter, in varying relationship, until amalgamation into the Territorial Force in 1907. Barnet Barracks were built in 1859-60 for the Herts and Middlesex Militias, and were demolished in 1989 for the Spires Shopping Centre.

The East and Chipping Barnet Volunteer Infantry was relatively short-lived, lasting from 1803-7, and also, with an establishment of 120, among the smaller of Hertfordshire's fifteen units. Its red uniform with blue facings and gold lace, though, yielded to none. During the same period, in 1805, the churchwardens and overseers of Hadley and South Mimms were ordered to provide one man between them for a Middlesex force and, after some delay, John Pickton 'who was residing with his Parents in an adjoining Parish

to Hadley, and about 20 years of Age entered as a Volunteer to serve for that Parish'.

It is nevertheless the Hertfordshire unit which is seen as the predecessor of the 12th Middlesex (Barnet) Rifle Battalion, raised during the next crisis, against the next Napoleon, in 1859. It had rifle ranges at Arkley and, initially, at Hadley. During the developing process of greater military integration, the 12th reluctantly lost its distinctive uniform – this time rifle green with black braiding and black 'Garibaldi' hats with long plumes of black cocks' feathers – in 1875, and in 1881 became part of the 7th Battalion Middlesex Regiment, one of the four Volunteer Battalions attached to the newly formed regular Middlesex Regiment. Their role was still that of home defence, but during the South African War members were invited to volunteer for active service, and many did so.

THE FIRST WORLD WAR

The militias and volunteer forces were combined in 1907 into a Territorial Force charged with home defence but intended to provide the means for expansion in a large-scale war. August 1914 therefore found the 7th Middlesex proud to be the first territorial battalion to leave for the front,

172. *The 7th Middlesex marching south through Barnet c.1900.*

although to its chagrin it had then to kick its heels instead in Gibraltar. Returning to England in February 1915 the men entrained for Barnet, where they went into billets and were sent home on leave in batches, before being sent in March to Flanders. From then until the Armistice they more than earned their share of the regulars' nickname, the Die-Hards.

Territorial regiments which went overseas could not fulfil their home defence role, and had therefore to raise reserve battalions. The 2/7th was recruited in September 1914, at Barnet until November before moving to Egham, and in Flanders by January 1915. Losses were so heavy that it was disbanded and merged in June 1916. The 3/7th was therefore raised, although there were already virtually no officers or NCOs to provide adequate training. It was at Barnet from March to May 1915, and was sent abroad (becoming the new 2/7th) in 1917. The 4/7th, whose training problems were even more acute, managed to remain a reserve battalion. The Territorial Force became the Territorial Army in 1920, and in the reorganisation of the 7th Middlesex the Hampstead and Barnet detachments were permanently disbanded.

Although its longstanding volunteer detachment was claimed for Middlesex, Barnet was also still part of Hertfordshire's defence system. In May 1915 a Herts Volunteer Regiment was formed, taking under its wing more than twenty local units. These were then divided into four battalions but, according to the regiment's historian, 'some difficulty was experienced in obtaining the necessary volunteers from the Barnet area to secure the independence of the 4th Battalion, and in 1916 it was absorbed into the 3rd Battalion as a single company'.

Whatever the reasons, they were not the fault of the New Barnet and District Volunteer Training Corps, which in May became the first, and only, two companies of the 4th Battalion. A rare set of its *Gazette* survives, from the first issue on 9 January 1915 to the sixty-eighth and last on 16 June 1916, and although the tone is rather more juvenile, the world it reveals comes close, in both its high courage and its parochialism, to that of Dad's Army. The *Gazette* records some of the difficulties of a group by definition excluded from regular service. Nevertheless it also shows the fashioning of an enthusiastic force, understandably proud of becoming part of the 4th Battalion.

In 1916 East Barnet Urban District, which had already granted a site for a shooting range, made an additional donation of up to £15 to 'enable the

173. *Some of the soldiers who passed through Arkley during the First World War.*

174. *The issue of the* Gazette *for 1 May 1915 which records the New Barnet and District Volunteer Training Corps'
transformation into the 4th Battalion Herts Volunteer Regiment.*

THE GAZETTE.

THE OFFICIAL ORGAN OF THE

4th Battalion Herts Volunteer Regiment.

President   -   -   The MARQUESS OF SALISBURY.

Vice=Presidents :

Sir CHARLES ALLOM, Col. H. TEMPEST HICKS, C.B., J.P., J. LOVELL PANK, Esq., D.L., J.P., E. NEWTON BUNGEY, Esq.,
H. HATFIELD, Esq., C. R. LEAR, Esq., F. MORTON JENNINGS, Esq., Councillor AMOS FORD, J.P., H. S. HOBSON. Esq.

General Council :

Messrs. A. G. WANE (Chairman and Treasurer), GAVIN SCOTT (Secretary), G. BAILEY, E. NEWTON BUNGEY,
E. A. CHAPPLE, E. CLARK, W. COOK, G. EMERY, C. EVERETT, W. W. GABELL, W. G. MUSSON, H. PEARCE,
E. W. PHILPOTT, T. H. ROURKE, W. STRINGER, and Councillor E. SMITH.

Headquarters : 63, EAST BARNET ROAD.

No. 15.   PRICE ONE PENNY.   1st MAY, 1915.

Editorial.—The Corps should be very proud of its new title. No longer is it the "New Barnet and District Vounteer Training Corps," but "4th Battalion Herts Volunteer Regiment." Without disdaining highly probable that we shall be used before very long, and we must show that the praise lavished on us by inspecting officers was well deserved.

Company Orders.

175. *The Barnet Workhouse Infirmary was extended to accommodate the wounded of the First World War.*

176. *Chipping Barnet's war memorial was unveiled on 3 April 1921, and moved to the churchyard on the far side of the church in 1937.*

Company to complete and equip the Range with modern up-to-date apparatus. The use of the Range will be extended to the Special Constables, who, like ourselves, are organised for Home Defence.' In June the Urban District Council promised to issue an appeal to every householder, followed up by personal visitation, that every man ineligible to join the army should join the Company. 'The Company has been given definite work to guard the railway....When the Council takes the lead it is hoped that the result will end in a little more local pride and enthusiasm for sacrifice and service'. This is an important reflection of the role of local government in wartime, one which would be greatly expanded in 1939 but would probably now be impossible. It also reflects some of the constant underlying tensions, a useful corrective to the assumption that all-out support for war efforts used always to be guaranteed.

The death-toll alone guaranteed that few escaped untouched by the First World War, but besides the constant, dreaded, telegrams, and the volunteer forces, local involvement was all-pervasive. Everyone saw the German airship shot down in 1916 by Lieutenant Leefe Robinson at Cuffley, and although air raids were still rare, black-out was enforced. The vast numbers of wounded meant that every available hospital, hall or large house was commandeered, and convalescents (as well as billeted soldiers) were plied with entertainment. Allotments and pig farms *(see p. 46)* flourished. The King of Prussia in Barnet High Street was renamed the King George.

The scale of death at the front is still marked by the war memorials, unveiled in every parish and in many schools and workplaces.

WORLD WAR II

Although in the event there was no invasion, improved airpower turned the Home Front in the 1939-45 war into an immediate reality. 334 Anti-Aircraft Company, Royal Engineers was formed at Barnet early in 1937 as a searchlight company of the 33rd (St Pancras) Anti-Aircraft Battalion. It trained locally both at the barracks and briefly in huts on the Cutbush nursery site which in 1937 became the Territorial Drill Hall. Local authority defence preparations took place through Air Raid Precautions (ARP, later called Civil Defence) committees, allied to wardens and the fire, ambulance and rescue services. Local firemen

177. Bomb damage in Osidge Lane, East Barnet, 1941.

helped the besieged capital, notably on the night when the London Docks burnt so fiercely that the light seemed local, and people stood in Hadley to watch the blaze. From the military side the next incarnation of volunteer forces, the Local Defence Volunteers (LDF), were raised in May 1940 and two months later had their name changed to Home Guard. The Women's Land Army had a hostel at The Oaks in Galley Lane (now the Poor Clares' convent) and the women travelled thence on foot or by bike to a wide variety of tasks, including hedging and ditching, potato lifting and sugar beet hoeing, stone picking at Folly Farm, cultivating crops at Barnet Sewage Works and Wrotham Park, and working in a munitions factory at Boreham Wood.

There was less bomb damage in Barnet and Hadley than in areas with more strategic targets, but insouciant small boys could all too easily make the usual shrapnel collections. In terms of total casualties, the worst V1 incident of the war occurred at STC on 23 August 1944, at 7.59am just as a shift was arriving, leaving 33 dead and 200 injured. The incidence maps are also comprehensively peppered, and there were various other fatalities and injuries, as well as irreparably damaged houses. Requisitioning, black-out, rationing and additional allotments returned. Arkley golf course was turned over to grazing, with the fairways restricted to a width of 30 yards and tended by one groundsman too old to serve; but its constant use by service personnel, whether stationed in the area or on leave, ensured no great damage.

On the national scale, local firms such as STC, Swains, Watson's and Maw's had precisely the expertise to make major contributions to the war

178. A group from the local Women's Land Army during the Second World War. Friendships forged during the war remained permanent thereafter.

effort. Both the telephone and radio branches of STC, for example, were heavily involved in the expansion of telecommunication for airborne, army and ARP systems, and two important components, high-grade selenium and ceramic buffer blocks, were manufactured at an out-station in Hadley Brewery.

The relatively open spaces near the St Albans Road sprouted both a dummy airfield, complete with empty huts and mock planes, and a real Prisoner of War camp (at the gate a model of Salzburg, lovingly made by its prisoners). Barnet Barracks hosted the Royal Army Pay Corps. Arkley hosted a subsidiary section of the secret code-breaking organisation based at Bletchley Park, whose existence was until recently a well-kept secret. In 1940 a key branch of M18c, or Radio Security Service, which did the actual interception of German military broadcasts, was transferred from London (actually Wormwood Scrubs) to a spacious house called Arkley View. Its high and uncluttered location made it ideal for radio interception, and other houses around – The Granary, Arkley Lodge, The Lawns, and Ravenscroft at Ravenscroft Park – were also requisitioned. A staff of 21 officers and 34 men were employed to pick up the messages, transcribe them, and send them four times a day by motor-cycle despatch rider to Bletchley Park for code-breaking. Shortly before D-Day the Arkley unit was also ordered to go proactive by transmitting misleading information, allegedly from General Patton's Fifth Army, placing the site of the allied landings near Calais rather than in Normandy.

PEACE CELEBRATIONS

Between the First and Second World Wars an elderly resident recounted one of his earliest recollections, being taken aged 7 by his father to see the decorations on Hadley Common to commemorate the end of the Crimean War in 1855: 'Over the gateway [to The Mount] an arch was made, covered with evergreens, and a great many red, white and blue crinkley bottles filled with oil, which looked very pretty among the evergreens'. Such arches were a feature of public celebrations in the 19th century, and other local examples are recorded for the relief of Mafeking as well as for royal occasions. In the 20th century bonfires became popular. They featured in the

peace celebrations after World War I at Folly Farm and Arkley, and also for such events as George V's jubilee, when the stocks at Hadley unfortunately added to the blaze. Children's street parties, one of the main ways of marking the end of World War II, were also much in evidence at Queen Elizabeth's coronation in 1953, and for subsequent royal celebrations up until now.

179. *One of the Christmas cards produced by U.A. Monck, a local ARP warden.*

180. *The bonfire for Arkley's celebrations at the end of the First World War.*

Index
Items marked with an asterisk
denote illustrations or captions

ABBEY FOLK PARK 130, *131
Acres, Birt 97-98
Act of Settlement 1662, 62
Adkins, John 128
'Admiral' buses 91
Aethelred II, King, 9
Agate 9, 10, 17, 43
Agriculture 38-50
Albert Road, New Barnet 107
Aleconners 32
Allen, Daniel 79
Allen, Elizabeth 112
Almshouses *41, 65-68
Alston Road 88, 97, 112
Alverstone Avenue 93
Amis, Kingsley 61
Angel public house, Enfield Chase 14
Anstee, Mr 44
Apprenticeships 62
Aps, Thomas 110
Archaeology 8, 43
Arkley 7, 10, 17, 18, 37, 44, 68, 91, 98, 139
Arkley Common 128
Arkley Lodge 139
Arkley Music Society 121
Arkey Villagers' Golf Club 128
Arkley windmill 43, *44
Arkley Working Men's Club 118
ARP 138, *140
Assembly Hall, Union Street *87
Assembly Rooms, Barnet High Street *34, 98, 120
Atkinson, Francis 56

BAKER'S FORGE *18
Baptists 76, *76, 79, 80
Barnard Heath 11
Barnet: boundaries 7, 8, 9-10, *9, *10, 11, 18; name derivation 11; ownership 7, 9
Barnet, London Borough of 18
Barnet & North Metropolitan Junction Railway 81
Barnet Amateur Dramatic Society 120
Barnet Amateur Orchestral Society 121
Barnet Amicable Society 68, 116-117
Barnet and District Local History Society 120
Barnet Arts Club 120
Barnet Association 27-28, 103
Barnet Barracks 134, 139
Barnet Blockhouse 14
Barnet Brewery 95
Barnet Cinema 129
Barnet College 114, *115
Barnet Common 22, 27, 36, 41, 44, 64, 86, 102, 121

Barnet Cricket Club 127
Barnet District Industrial Exhibitions 79, 118, *118, 121
Barnet District Industrial Star 118
Barnet Fairs 22-27, *22, *23, *24, *25, *26, 103
Barnet Football Club 97, 128-129, *128
Barnet Gate 9, 10, 11, 13, 13, *30, 38, 44
Barnet High Street 10, *10, 14-15, *14, 19, 21, *22, 33, 34, *35, 44, *46, 50, 64, 76, *76, 95, *82, *99, *100, *101, *104, 105, 121, 125, *126, *135
Barnet Hill 8, 14, 15, 23, 33, 43, *107, 111
Barnet Horticultural and Floricultural Society 116, *116, *117
Barnet Hospital 65, 97, 108
Barnet manor 7, 9-10, *9, *10, 18, *30
Barnet Market 17, 19-21, *19, *20, *21, 50, 106
Barnet Militia 134, *134
Barnet Motor Services 91
Barnet Museum 120
Barnet Natural History Society 119
Barnet Press 27, 116, 119
Barnet Provident Club 120, *120
Barnet Races 27, *27
Barnet Record Society 98, 119-120
Barnet Rural Sanitary District 18
Barnet Temperance Council 89
Barnet Theatre 120
Barnet Town Band 121, *122
Barnet Town Hall *8, 88, 98
Barnet Union Society 68
Barnet Urban Sanitary District 18
Barnet Ventilator 97
Barnetley 17
Bates, Richard 14
Bath Place 21, 91, 97
Battle of Barnet 41, 131-32
Battle of Barnet obelisk *15, *131, 132
Baxter, Richard 74, 88
Beacon Hill 43, 132
Beacon House 56
Beacons 8, 132, *133
Bean, Cosmo 127
Bear, dancing *123
Beating the Bounds 8, *8
Beauchamp, John 69-70, *70
Bedford Avenue 27
Bell, Walter 37
Bell public house, Barnet Gate *13
Bell's Hill 97
Bell's Lane 88
Belle Vue 60
Belmont 58, *59, 127
Belmont Avenue 92
Belmont estate 93
Bennett, A.T. 91
Berriman, Joseph 23
Berrowe, Anne 74
Betstile 9, 10, 52
Bevan estate *93, 95
Black, Alice 102

Black Death 29
Black Horse public house *83
Blishen, Edward 101
Bohun family 38
Bohun Lodge 56, 58, 79
Bomb damage 138, *138
Booth, William 79
Boscawen, Frances 52, 53
Bourn Lodge 58
Boxing 25, 121-122, 125
Boys, W. Osborn 22
Boys' Farm Home 113, *113
Brent river 9
Breweries 95
Brickfields 44
British Land Co. 84, 85
British Legion *121
British Schools 112
Broade, John 102
Browne, J. Harris 95
Brunswick Park 85
Brunswick Park Road 52, 106
Brunt, William 62
Buckskin Hall 58, *59
Bull inn 23, 68, 102
Bulls Head 33, 88
Burnaby, J.D. 127
Burney, Fanny 53
Burrows, John, 52, 53
Buses 81, 91
Butchers' Company 20
Butterfield, William 70, 72
Byfield, Dora 120
Byng family 33, 61
Byng Road 112

CAPEL ROAD 93
Carnarvon Road 88
Carr, Robert 61
Carriers 32
Cars 125, *126
Cass, Frederick 58
Castle, The 88
Cat Hill 13, 46, 57, 68, *68, 88
Cattley, William 56
Chandos, Dukes of 39, 41
Chapone, Hester 53, 55, *55
Charity schools 112
Chase, The, Hadley 61
Chesterfield estate 95
Children's Nursing Home and Hospital 108, 109, *109
Cholera 106
Christ Church, Barnet 77, *78, 80
Christ Church, Cockfosters 78, 106
Church Farm Industrial School 113, *113
Church Hill House 52, 56, 58
Church Hill Road 13, 57, *57
Church Passage 98
Churches 69-80
Cinema Palace 129, *129
Cinemas 129
Cinematography 97-98, *98
Circuses 25, *119
Clark, Henry, nurseryman 50

Clarke, Sir Simon *113
Clock and Watchmakers' Asylum 67, *67
Clock House *18, 58, *58
Clockhouse Parade *58
Coaches 21, *31, 32
Cock, The *11
Cockfosters 7, 58
Cockfosters Bowling Club 127
Cockfosters Cricket Club 127
Cockfosters estate 95
Cockfosters Tennis Club 127
Commercial Hotel 34
Commons 41-42
Community (Institute) of St Andrew 77, 114
Congregationalists 74-75, *74, *75, 79, 80, *85
Conyers Park 95
Cooke, John 102
Cornwell's nursery 50
Council housing 93, 95
Cowing's 98, *100
Cowley College 114
Cox's Dairy 46, *46
Cricket 125, *126, 127
Crime 102
Cromer Road 96
Crouch, Richard 34
Cutbush, William 50
Cycling *11, 124-125, *125

DACRE LODGE 58
Dairy farming 46, *47
Defoe, Daniel 37
Delany, Mary 53
Dickens, Charles 33, 110
Dollis Brook 10
Dominion, East Barnet Road 129
Dove, George 25
Dowling, Fred *101
Duck's Island, Mays Lane 78
Dudmans (house) 58
Duke of York public house, Gannick Corner 124
Dunsford, Charles 91
Dury family 55
Dury House 55
Dury Road 43
Dyke Cottage, Arkley 43
Dyrham Park 45, 77

EARL'S DAIRY, Hadley Farm *47
East and Chipping Barnet Volunteer Infantry 134
East Barnet 17, *18, 93
East Barnet Gas and Water Company 106-107, *107
East Barnet manor house 53
East Barnet National School 46
East Barnet Road 85, 91
Eastern Counties Railway 81
Easton's Nursery 50
Edgware, Highgate & London Railway Co. 81, 83
Edmonton 10, 12, 39

Effendi, Shogi 85
Electricity 107
Elizabeth I, Queen 51
Elliott & Son 97, *97
Elm Farm, Galley Lane 46
Emmerton's nursery *49, 50
Enclosure 42, *42, 43, 86
Enfield 7, 9, 12, 38, 39
Enfield Chase 10, 12, 38-41, *38, 43, 59, 121
Erysipelas 106
Essoldo 129
Etheridge, Sydney 127
Eu, Hugh de 12
Eversley estate 68

FALDO, John 75
Fields, Gracie 129
Fiennes, Celia 37, 75
Fire fighting 105, *105
Fishmongers' Company 36
Fitzjohn Avenue 91, *92
Flashman, Stan 129
Folly Farm 46, *48
Foot racing 124, *124
Football *127, 128-129, *128
Foundlings 108
Fox, George 74
Fox-hunting 121
Francis, car dealers *126
Fremlin's 95
Frowyk family 43, 51, *51
Frusher, Cllr 46, 49
Fry, Barry 129
Fuller, Thomas 36
Fulwood, Alice 102

GALLANTS FARM estate 93
Galley Lane 46, 138
Gambling 27-28
Gannick Corner 14, 124
Garden party *117
Garrett, John 66
Garrett's almshouses 66
Garrow, David, 113
Gas supplies 106-107, *107
Gaumont cinema 129
Gelder, Bill 120
Geology 7-8, *7
George IV, King 121
Gill, Ralph 58
Gillum, Lt. Col. 113
Gladmore Heath 41
Glebe Farm 39
Golf 127-128
Gordon Riots 52
Grady, Nicholas 121
Granary, The 139
Grange estate 95
Granville Road 88, 108
Grasvenor Avenue 66
Grasvenor estate 91
Grazing 44-45
Great North Road 10, 14-17, *15, *16, 102
Great Northern Railway 81, 83-84

Great Northern Railway Cemetery 85, *86
Green Belt 91
Green Dragon public house 88
Green Man public house *17, 21, 33, *33, 34, 121
Green, Reginald 121
Greenhill Grove/Park (house) 57, *57, 60, 68
Greenhill Park estate 93
Grendel's Gate 11, 17, *30
Grimsdyke Crescent 50
Grocott Cottages 91, *92

HADLEY: boundaries 7; name derivation 11; ownership 7
Hadley Beacon/Cresset 132, *133
Hadley Brewery *94, 95, *103
Hadley Common 10, 39, *40, 113, 127
Hadley family 54, *54
Hadley Green 41, *41, *109
Hadley Hall 130
Hadley Hermitage 70
Hadley Highstone 12, 39, *47, 50, *50, 78, 86, *87, 91, *92, 97, 98, 106, 107
Hadley Infant School *109
Hadley Lodge 61
Hadley manor house 51
Hadley Memorial Hall 118
Hadley Rectory *52
Hadley Ridge estate 91
Hadley Wood station 91
Hale, William 73, *73
Harrow School 50
Harts Horns public house 33, 88
Harvey, T. Morgan 79
Harwood, Mary 102
Hasluck, Lancelot 68, *68
Hasluck almshouses 68
Hatton, Jesse 27
Haymaking 45, *45
Hendon Wood Lane 10, 13
Hermitage, Hadley 12
High Barnet station 84, *84
Highstone School *112
Highwaymen 33, 102
Hippodrome cinema 129
Hodges, Samuel 76
Hoggy Lane 21
Holy Trinity Guild 30, 32, 69-70, 72, 110
Holy Trinity, Lyonsdown 78
Homelessness 62
Horticulture 49, *49, 57, 116
Hoskin, William 102
Hospitals 56, 65, *65, 66, 97, 108
Howard, Elizabeth Jane 61
Hurst Cottage, Hadley 61

INDEPENDENTS 74-75, *74, 76
Inns and alehouses 32-4, 88
Institute (Community) of St Andrew, Wood Street 77, 114
Irish in Barnet 45

JACK, Charles 41

Jackson, William 92
Jackson Road *92, 93
Jenkins, E.H. 110
Jesus Hospital charity 66, *66
Johnson's Pharmaceuticals 96

KENTISH TOWN 66, 76
Kimpton, William 38-9, *39
King's Head public house 125
Kitchener, William 33
Kitson, Peter 10, 12
Kitts End 45, 76
Knightley, John 66
Knights Hospitaller 20
Knott, George 56

LANDON, Letitia Elizabeth 53
Latimer's Elm *52, 73, *73
Lawns, The 139
Leathersellers' Company almshouses 66, *67, *83
Leecroft Road 66
Leftwich, B.R. 119
Lemmons, Hadley 61
Lewkenor, Sir Roger de 18
Linacres, William 20
Line, Joseph 121
Lipton, Thomas 54, *54
Little Grove 51, 53, 56, 57, 58
Little Larkins 95
Livingstone, David 55, *55
Livingstone Cottage *55
Lloyd, William 76
Lollards 72
London, Bishop of 9
London & General Omnibus Co. 91
London Passenger Transport Board 91
Longmore Avenue 13, 84
Lower Red Lion *16, 33, 34, *34
Lyonsdown 60
Lyonsdown estate 84
Lyonsdown Middle-Class School 113
Lyonsdown Photographic Society 98
Lyonsdown Road 85
Lytton Road *86
Lytton Road Assembly Rooms 129

MACHYN, Henry 73
Mail coaches *31, 32, 33
Mandeville de family 7, 11, 12, 38, 70
Manor Cottage 97
Manor Road 46, 86, *88, 91
Market – see Barnet Market
Market gardens 49-50
Market Place 21, *127, 128
Marriott Road 89
Marryat, Thomas 75
Mary Payne's Place 21, *22
Maudling, Reginald 61
Maw's, Cromer Road 96, 138
Mays Lane 13, 27, 46, 78, 86, 91, 95
Meadway 25, *82, 91
Meadway estate 27
Mendoza, Daniel 121
Methodists 76, *76, 79, 80

Metropolitan Electric Tramways 89
Middle Row 19, *19, 20
Middlesex Regiment 134
Mildmay Mission 77, 109
Mill Corner 43, 91
Milling 43
Mimms Side 50
Missionaries 24-25, 45, 64
Mitre public house 121, 122, 123
Monk, General 133, *133
Monkenfrith, East Barnet 52, 60
Monken Hadley Cricket Club 127
Monkenholt, Hadley 61
Monro family 56
Montagu, Elizabeth 53
Mount House, Hadley 12, 39, 114
Mount Pleasant 58, *59
Moxon Street 82, 86, 112
Municipal piggery 46, *48
Mutual aid societies 68

NATIONAL SCHOOLS 112, 113
Nesbitts Alley 97
Neville, Richard Earl of Warwick 131-132
New Barnet 60, 84-85, *85
New Barnet Gas and Water Co. 125
New Barnet Literary and Debating Society 118, 120
New Barnet Picture Theatre 129
New Barnet station 81, *81
New Barnet Young Men's Mutual Improvement Society 118
New Southgate 9
New Southgate Cemetery and Crematorium 85, *86
Newman, Thomas 34
Noble, Ralph 74
Normandy Avenue 25, 34, 91
Norrysbury, Cockfosters 58
North Metropolitan Power Distribution Co. 107
North Road Boxing Club 125
Northaw 38
Northern Line 84
Northern Photographic Works 97
Northumberland Road 10
Nurseries 49, *49
Nursery Row 50

OAKFIELD AVENUE 44
Oakhill (house) 57, 59-60, *59
Oakhill Park 127
Oakhurst Avenue 93
Oakleigh Park 81
Oaks, The, Galley Lane 138
Obelisk *15, *131, 132
Odeon, Underhill 129, *130
Old Bull Theatre 120
Old Fold 12, *13, 38, *45, 51, 61
Old Fold Manor Golf Club 128
Olney, Billie 23, 25, 45, 46
Olney, Cllr 23, 98
Osborne, Diana 36
Osidge 38, 54, *54, 57, 60

Osidge Lane *138
Ossulton Convalescent Home 109, *109
Owen, John 36

PAGITT, Justinian 65
Pagitt's almshouses 65, *65
Palmer, Eleanor 66
Palmer's almshouses 66
Papworth, John Buonarotti 58, 60
Park Road, New Barnet 97, 108, 114, 130
Parkbridge Nurseries, Park Road 91
Parker, Henry 51
Pawling, Katherine 108
Peace celebrations 139-140, *140
Peasants' Revolt 30
Pennefather, William 24, 77-78, 109
Pennefather Hall 77-78, *78
Pepys, Samuel 33, 36, 120
Pepys, Sir William 53
Pepys Crescent 37
Pevsner, Nikolaus 61
Philip's Group 97
Phoenix Brewery 95
Physic Well 36-37, *36, *37
Piccadilly Line 93
Pickton, John 134
Pigs 46
Plank, Mr 25
Pleasant Sunday Afternoon *87, 89
Policing 102-105, *104
Poor Law Act 1601, 62
Poor Law Amendment Act 1834, 62
Poor relief 62-68
Poorhouses 63, *63
Population 93
Postal services 32, 33, 34
Potter, Christina le 44
Potteries 43, *43
Potters Lane 13, 66, 84
Presbyterians 79
Prevost, General 60
Price, John 133
Pricklers 60
Pricklers Hill 60
Prince of Wales, East Barnet 91
Priory, The 60, *60
Prittle family 60
Private schools 113
Public Health Act 1872, 18
Pymlicoe House, Hadley 61
Pymmes Brook 10, 13, *13, 17, 57, 105

QUAKERS 76
Queen Elizabeth's School for Boys 37, 66, 76, 110-111, *110, 112
Queen Elizabeth's Girls' School *107, 111
Queen's Arms 88, *89
Queen's Head 88
Queens Road 88

RACE COURSE 25, 27, *27, 121
Ragged School 112
Railways 21, 22, 27, 32, 81-85

Raincliffe Ladies' College 114, *115
Ravenscourt Park 42, *42
Ravenscourt Park estate 42
Ravenscroft James 66, 78
Ravenscroft, Thomas 78, *78
Ravenscroft almshouses 66
Ravenscroft Gardens 23
Ravenscroft Park estate 88
Raydean Road 127
Rea, Charles *16, *77
Rea, Richard 59
Red Lion 25, 28, *29, *32, 33, 34, *34, 45, 81, 116, 120, 121 (*see also Lower Red Lion*)
Redehede, William 14
Redhead, William 72
Reformation 73-74
Regal cinema 129
Ripley, James 28, *28
Road maintenance 14
Roads (main) 13, 14, 17
Robinson's grocers *101
Rodford, Michael 57
Roman Catholics 76-77
Roman roads 13, 14
Romans 8, 14
Rosslyn Avenue 93
Rowlands, William 67
Rowley 10, 11, 17, 18
Rowley Green Road 44
Russell Lane estate 93

SAINSBURY'S, Barnet High St. 101
St Albans Abbey 7, 9, 18, 19, 29, 30, 72
St Albans Road 16, 19, 34, 50, 86
St James, New Barnet 112
St John, Barnet 7, *14, *15, *31, 69-70, 72, *72, 74
St Mary, East Barnet 18, 69, *69, 70
St Mary, Hadley 56, *56, 70, *70, *71, 132
St Peter, Arkley 77, *77
St Peter's Players 120
St Stephen, Bell's Hill 78, *98
St Wilfrid's Road 95
Salisbury Arms 34, 88, *117, 127, *129
Salisbury Road 97
Salvation Army 79, *79, 80
Sanders, Thomas 125
Sanger, George, circus *119
Sayers, Tom 25
Scarlet fever 106
Schools 46, *109, 110-115
Scot, Thomas 133
Searche, Robert 20
Sebright Road *100
Sewerage 105-106, *106
Shadd, Alice 14
Sharpe, John 56
Sharpe, Mary 53
Sharpe's Farm, Underhill 46
Shaw, Samuel 74
Shepherd's, butchers *99
Shops 98, 101
Silesia College 114, *114
Smith, Henry 62
Smith, Thomas 42

Smith's bakery, Hadley *41
Smith-Bosanquet, Major 121
Smyth, John 102
Society of Friends 76
South Mimms 12, 14, 18, 39, 76
Southaw 38
Southaw Wood 43
Southgate 10
Southgate Borough Council 127
Spires, The, shopping centre 10, *10, 134
Spurr, Alexander 85
Standard Telephones and Cables 96, *96, 138
Stanhope 95
Stapylton Road 88
Star Tavern (Coffee House) *82, 83
Station Road, New Barnet 85, 91, 114
Stevens, William *34, 98
Stocks 103, *103
Strafford family 109
Strafford Road 88
Street, G. E. 70
Stuart, Lady Arabella 51, *52
Sunday schools 77
Sutton & Co. 66
Swain, John Co. 21, 97, *97, 138
Swimming 125

TABAR 34
Tapster Street 86
Tavern Hill *85
Taylor, E. Fergusson 129
Temperance 89
Tempest, Mrs 57
Territorial Drill Hall 50, 138
Thackeray, William Makepeace 53
Thomas Watson Homes 66
Thornton, Richard 66
Thornton's Almshouses 66, *67
Three Horseshoes public house 88
Tidmarsh, H.E. 88-89
Toldervy, William 27, 33
Traffic congestion 14, 15, *15
Trams 89, *90, 91
Trent Park 120, 127
Trevor family 58
Trevor Hall 58
Trevor Lodge *57, 58
Trevor Park 113
Trinder, Dr William 37, *37
Trolleybuses 89, 91
Trollope, Anthony 53
Trotter, Captain John 24, 64, 77
Tudor Hall *110
Tudor House *104
Turner J.M.W. 56
Turner, Ely 74
Turnpike roads 14
Two Brewers, Hadley 12, 88, 91, 125, *125
Typhoid 105, 106

UDNY, Robert 56
Underhill *16, 22, 34, *34, 46, 88, *89, 106, 128
Underhill playing fields 127

Union Street 65, 76, 86, *87, 88, 98, 112
United Reform Church 75, *75

VAGRANTS 62
Vernon Crescent 10
Verulam Lodge Establishment for Young Ladies 114
Victoria Cottage Hospital 56, 66, *107, 108, *108
Victoria Lane 125
Volunteer regiments 134-135, *135

WAITROSE 98, 129
Walden Abbey 7, 11, 39, 70, 72
Walsh, Michael 102
War memorial *137
Ward, John 130
Warren & Co. coal merchants 79
Warwick Nursery 50, *50
Warwick's Oak 132, *132
Water supplies 105, 107
Watson, Thomas 66
Watson's 97, 138
Welch, Michael 102
Welch family *100
Well Road 37
Wellhouse estate 37, 95
Well-house Farm 37
Wellington public house *33, 88
Wesley, John 76
Wesleyan chapel, Barnet High St. *10
West Farm, Cockfosters 58
Whalebones, Wood Street 98
Whetstone and Highgate Turnpike Trust 14, *16, 17
Whitbread's 95
White Bear public house 34
White Hart public house 116
White Horse public house 88
Whitings Hill 95
Wilbraham, Sir Roger 65
Wilbraham's almshouses *41, 65
Willenhall 60
Windmill public house Hadley 12, 43, *43
Windmills 43
Women's Land Army 138, *139
Wood Street 13, *14, 23, 32, 34, *35, 50, 56, 66, *74, 75, 76, 77, *83, 86, 95, *108, 114, 120
Woodcock Farm estate 85
Woolpack public house *32, 33, 45, 68, 88
Workhouses 63-65, *63, *65, *137
World War I 56, 49, 134-135, *136, *137, 138
World War II *108, 138-139, *138, *139
Wrotham Cottage 97
Wrotham Park 61, 109, 120
Wyatt, Thomas 60
Wyld, William 76

YMCA 125
Yonge, Juliana 53, 55
Young, Arthur 39, 44
Young Men's Association 118